Tips

SCOTLAND

SCOTLAND NORWAY
Glasgow Edinburgh
IRELAND DENMARK
Dublin GREAT North Sea
BRITAIN
London NETHER-
LANDS
GERMANY
BELG.
FRANCE LUX.

D0716098

SYMBOLS

INSIDER TIP   Insider Tip

★   Highlight

●●●●   Best of ...

❄   Scenic view

☺   Responsible travel: fair trade principles and the environment respected

(*)   Telephone numbers that are not toll-free

PRICE CATEGORIES HOTELS

Expensive   over 120 pounds

Moderate   75–120 pounds

Budget   under 75 pounds

The prices are for a double room, for one night, with breakfast

PRICE CATEGORIES RESTAURANTS

Expensive   over 30 pounds

Moderate   15–30 pounds

Budget   under 15 pounds

The prices are for a three course meal without drinks

On the cover: Highland Games in Braemar p. 22 and p. 107 | St Kilda: an unspoilt natural paradise p. 78

CONTENTS

The Highlands → p. 62

The West Coast & Hebrides → p. 76

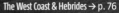

Orkney & Shetland → p. 86

Road atlas → p. 118

MAPS IN THE GUIDEBOOK

(120 A1) Page numbers
and coordinates refer to
the road atlas

(0) Site/address located off
the map

(U A1) Refers to the street
map of Edinburgh inside the
back cover

Street map of Glasgow
→ p. 134/135

INSIDE BACK COVER:
PULL-OUT MAP →

PULL-OUT MAP

(A–B 2–3) Refers to the
removable pull-out map

(a–b 2–3) Refers to the
additional inset maps on the
pull-out map

The best MARCO POLO Insider Tips

Our top 15 Insider Tips

INSIDER TIP **Loch tête-à-tête**
Rendezvous with nature: before you say a toast on the shore of Loch Skeen, you first need to scramble up along the waterfall → **p. 35**

INSIDER TIP **Creepy castle**
Hermitage Castle in the Border country resembles the backdrop to a gloomy Shakespeare film: atmospheric and sinister → **p. 35**

INSIDER TIP **Art al fresco**
Glenkiln Reservoir is home to some authentic sculptures by Auguste Rodin, Henry Moore and other big names that embellish the four mile footpath along the reservoir → **p. 39**

INSIDER TIP **Never-ending story**
Prose and poetry is alive and well at the Scottish Storytelling Centre based at John Knox House on Edinburgh's Royal Mile. The house of the Scottish reformer is the most splendid on the Royal Mile → **p. 54**

INSIDER TIP **Take a city jog!**
Edinburgh is narrow and there are stairs everywhere so your best bet for a good run is along the River Leith → **p. 55**

INSIDER TIP **Best of Scottish produce**
20 years later and the Grain Store is still the best spot to have a meal in the historic Old Town part of Edinburgh → **p. 58**

INSIDER TIP **Eclectic shopping**
Brand shopping on Edinburgh's main boulevards can be expensive so why not try the Grassmarket's small independent stores in Old Town → **p. 59**

INSIDER TIP **Eco hostel on a loch**
The eco-friendly Loch Ossian youth hostel is right in the middle of the moors with no access by road but if you ask, the train conductor will drop you off at Corrour Station about a mile's walk away. There are no showers but there is hot water → **p. 67**

BEST OF ...

FOR FREE

● *Enjoy a smorgasbord extraordinaire*

Renowned paintings, a Royal Air Force Spitfire, stuffed giraffes, contemporary art: it is seldom that you will find such an entertaining mix under one roof. At Glasgow's *Kelvingrove Art Gallery & Museum* you get to see them all without even having to pay a penny → p. 45

● *Picnic in front of a Renaissance façade*

If you want to go inside the atmospheric ruins of *Caerlaverock Castle* there is an entrance fee. However, sitting on the lawns surrounding the fortress moat is free of charge and a picnic especially at dusk, with the ancient walls a special hue, can be ever so romantic → p. 38

● *Under tropical palms*

Edinburgh's *Royal Botanic Garden* is home to Great Britain's largest Victorian greenhouse dating back to 1858. This alone makes it worth a visit, as do the Scottish Highlands in miniature → p. 56

● *Chapel at the end of the world*

Homesick and seeking solace: this is what prompted Italian prisoners of war to build the *Italian Chapel* on the remote Orkney Islands during World War Two. This symbol of peace and reconciliation still moves visitors to this day → p. 87

● *Enigmatic stones*

Sunrise over the *Callanish Standing Stones* (photo) on the Isle of Lewis will catapult you back nearly 5000 years. Made of Lewisian gneiss, the sensation of standing solitary among them at the dawn of a new day is priceless → p. 78

● *Haunting cemeteries*

Let the story of 19th century body snatchers, Burke and Hare, make the hairs stand up on your arms in Edinburgh's sombre *Greyfriars Cemetery* with accounts of how they dug up fresh corpses and sold them to the university's school of anatomy. And in Glasgow's necropolis admire the colossal collection of tombstones of important citizens → p. 46 and 55

●●●● Dots in guidebook refer to 'Best of ...' tips

● *Edinburgh's magnificent mile*

The *Royal Mile* is a stretch where you will find all
things Scottish and along the way you go from
the 21st century all the way back to the Middle
Ages. The strains of the bagpipe, ghost walks
and quaint pubs all set the tone for your
Scotland stay → p. 57

● *Nessie mania*

Steve Feltham has been tracking the *Loch
Ness* monster since 1991. A full time Nessie
hunter, he lives on the famous loch and is
always keen to share what knowledge he
has of the mythical sea serpent → p. 96

● *Legendary hiking trail*

A trip to the Highlands wouldn't be complete with-
out this hike: the *West Highland Way* from Glasgow to
Fort William is just less than 95 miles long and is legendary.
Outlaw Rob Roy once hid in the idyllic wooded eastern shore of Loch
Lomond → p. 71

● *A whisky pilgrimage*

Only the Scottish could succeed in harnessing the spirit and taste of
their country in a bottle! For connoisseurs there is the *Malt Whisky Trail*
and you get to taste your way through the distilleries sip by sip → p. 75

● *Sit! Stay! Good dog!*

At *Viv Billingham's* on St Mary's Loch and on *Leault Farm* at Aviemore
you can watch the clever Scottish Border collies hard at work → p. 37
and 70

● *Royal Highland Games*

To see men in skirts tossing the caber or country dancing you should
visit one of Scotland's many folk festivals. The guys are absolute pros!
If you attend the main one in *Braemar* you could even get a glimpse
of the Queen and her family → p. 22 and 107

● *Folk music to get you going*

Celtic folk music is both melancholic and haunting and yet also very
danceable. *Sandy Bell's* is an Edinburgh pub where it is played and sung
at jam sessions – also at the Orkney and Shetland festivals (photo)
→ p. 60 and 106

ONLY IN

BEST OF ...

● *Celtic pub stop*
The Ceilidh Place, a café-style restaurant in Ullapool, has a great bookstore and such a homely atmosphere that you won't mind whiling away some time until the sun comes out → p. 84

● *Rune graffiti*
The Vikings sought refuge in *Maes Howe* on Orkney and left behind intriguing runes that they carved into the chamber walls: interesting enough to take your mind off the rain (photo) → p. 88

● *Cross country by train*
Watch the magnificent landscape of mountains, moors and lakes race by as the rain patters down. All from the comfort of your train carriage – the *West Highland Line* to Fort William is just one of many routes → p. 98

● *Gothic Revival architecture*
A pristine white Carrara marble chapel, a bedchamber with a ceiling with constellations and planets, an entrance hall like a church ... *Mount Stuart House* on the Isle of Bute is the epitome of Scottish neo-Gothic design and perfect for a rainy day → p. 50

● *Snug under the turf*
What can be cosier than watching the storms and lashing rains from the comforts of a luxuriously furnished cottage with expansive panoramic windows? Book into the turf-roofed *Blue Reef Cottages* that nestle into the hillside on the dramatic Harris coast → p. 79

● *Fun science*
Travel to the stars or to the intriguing world of Alice in Wonderland, observe cockroaches in captivity or be turned into a giant. The exhibits, Imax cinema and planetarium at the *Glasgow Science Centre* will provide lots of entertainment → p. 45

RAIN

RELAX AND CHILL OUT
Take it easy and spoil yourself

● *Heavenly repose*
Wake up well rested in a four-poster bed, spend unhurried hours in front of the fireplace, enjoy the view of the Highlands from your wing chair with a glass of wine in hand – *Darroch Learg Hotel* is just one of many Scottish manor houses and castles offering stylish relaxation → **p. 65**

● *Unwind at a city spa*
The *Sheraton Grand Hotel* spa in Edinburgh is a good place for hours of relaxation with its Turkish bath, saunas and variety of treatments not to mention a huge rooftop swimming pool → **p. 60**

● *In the mood for an ayurvedic massage?*
Treat yourself to this rejuvenating massage which is par for the course at the award-winning spa at the *Gleneagles Golf Resort*. You can enjoy the whole repertoire of wellness treatments from a crystal steam bath to a hot stone massage (photo) in elegant surrounds characterised by wood, leather and luxurious fabrics → **p. 72**

● *Twilight hours in Edinburgh*
Head up *Calton Hill* at twilight to Edinburgh's own Athenian acropolis, it offers one of the most magnificent views of the capital city. Lean against one of the pillars, relax and enjoy the view and don't forget to take along sundowners → **p. 54**

● *Far from the madding crowd*
Want to get away from it all for a day or so? Do as David Bowie and Leonhard Cohen have done in the past and visit *Holy Island* and re-energise in its spiritual centre and Buddhist retreat. The mandala garden is lovely → **p. 50**

● *A Garden of Eden*
Of all of Scotland's gardens the *Inverewe Gardens* at Ullapool in the far north has to be the most stunning. Enjoy this sub-tropical paradise that is so very unusual for this part of the world → **p. 85**

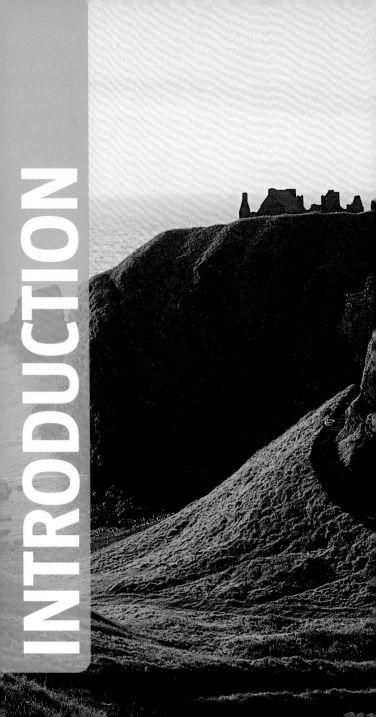

INTRODUCTION

DISCOVER SCOTLAND!

Scotland is iconic! Nessie and whisky, bagpipes, castles and myths lure you to this wildly romantic northern country with its magnificent, scenic landscapes. On a drive through the countryside you will be rewarded with panoramic views of hills, bog lakes and steep coastlines. The Atlantic weather ensures constant changes in the sky's hue and the dramatic Highlands are at their most spectacular on foot. Scotland's exceptional natural environment and changeable weather has left an indelible mark on its people. Their disposition has been influenced as much by historic hardship, a subarctic location and strict Calvinistic values, as by the fierce and melancholic character of their ancestors: the Celts, Scots and Picts. It is this blend that has resulted in the Scots being more frank and impetuous than their more reserved southern neighbours, the Anglo-Saxon English. No wonder these two different temperaments cannot find common ground! However, since Scotsmen Tony Blair and Gordon Brown were prime ministers, and Scotland was once again permitted a Scottish parliament, there has been greater understanding among the two nations.

Photo: Dunnottar Castle near Aberdeen

The five million Scots, who live in an area roughly the size of Austria, can be confident about their future. Ship building on the River Clyde may have been key to getting Scotland's economy up to speed 150 years ago, but today its primary growth is in computer and genetic engineering in the 'Silicon Glen' between Edinburgh and Glasgow. University places in Scotland are highly sought after and the country has been able to rely on innovation and an excellent education system for a long time now.

Real men wear skirts

Its natural landscape is what draws most visitors to Scotland but it is also a cultural destination. In the lovely southern Lowlands small towns like Jedburgh or Peebles and their Romanesque 12th century abbey ruins draw in visitors, their Gothic arches bearing testimony to Scotland's border history. A bicycle tour or day hike (e.g. in Melrose) is the best way to see the country's monastery ruins and trout rivers. Abbotsford House on the River Tweed is a must and will also put you on the trail of Scotland's literature. In the 19th century it was the fairy-tale residence of novelist Sir Walter Scott, to whom Scotland and the Highlands owe their fame abroad. Without Sir Walter's stories, the cliché of men in tartan kilts would never have captured the public's imagination. There would be no Hollywood Highlander without the Lowlander Scott; the curtain would never have been raised on Donizetti's opera 'Lucia di Lammermoor'. That said, there are many Scottish legends that are not due to Sir Walter: the legend of the Loch Ness monster; the strains of the bagpipes; the taste of distilled whisky and the charm of Sean Connery in all his 007 glory.

Glasgow and Edinburgh line up between the Lowlands and the Highlands forming a natural border. These two cites, separated by only an hour's rail journey, could not be more different. Edinburgh exudes a picturesque charm, especially its Royal Mile. One of Europe's most atmospheric promenades, its rankings often reach Mediterranean highs. Locals sit in its outdoor cafés in their shirtsleeves after work while curious tourists explore its alleyways. The narrow lanes and alleys are quite spooky at dusk making it easy to imagine the past witch hunts and the escapades of Dr. Jekyll and Mr. Hyde. Glasgow is quite different. Here the city's façade does not look as though it has been hewn from a single mould; instead neo-classical temples vie for attention among neo-Gothic towers and art nouveau influences. If you go for a drive, the street layout is more like that of Chicago than something out of the Middle Ages. In Glasgow

6000 BC
Mesolithic hunters and gatherers come across a land bridge to the island

500 BC
Celtic tribes move into the area known as Scotland today

843
Kenneth MacAlpine crowned first King of the Scots at Scone

1296
Scotland becomes an English province

1297
William Wallace (Braveheart) expelled the English in the Battle of Stirling – he was later betrayed by Scottish nobility and executed in 1305

The iron railway bridge across the Firth of Forth near Edinburgh

you will experience the Scottish way of life and temperament at its authentic best. Though the dialect may even have English speakers flummoxed, the street life, the music clubs, the exciting art scene and the hospitality are bound to enthral.

The Highlands begin north of the cities, a velvet green mountainous region reminiscent of places like Sardinia or Patagonia. Here the *lochs*, or lakes, shine like mirrors between the high mountains or *bens*. The

The Highlands feel like Patagonia

lakes are the territory of trout fishermen, while the rivers are for the salmon fishermen. When travelling by car, everywhere you look are the most magnificent vistas, no matter where the road takes you. To your left you may have rolling mist creeping across the peat bog while to the right you may see the reddish hide of a Highland bull gleaming against the pink heather. For just a moment sun rays may catch an isolated group of pine trees in the middle of a lake, before briefly touching the slope of a

1314
Robert the Bruce defeated the English at Bannockburn and declared Scotland independent

1542–87
The era of Mary Queen of Scots. After an unsuccessful attempt to regain the throne she was beheaded by Queen Elizabeth I.

1692
The Glencoe Massacre led to the death of 78 MacDonald clan members. Their descendants travel to Glencoe on 13 February to commemorate the event

1707
Act of Union: the Scottish Parliament decides on a union with England

jagged peak where eagles and ravens circle. The sea is never more than an hour's drive away. On the rough and rugged west coast, between Oban and Mallaig, the sky turns from turquoise to pink in the evening. In the east, across the small harbour of the Fife peninsula, the typical morning sea fog, the *haar*, clears up to reveal a Mediterranean-like sky. For the Scottish a round of golf in these surrounds is part and parcel of their everyday life. Visitors and even beginners should really give it a go. Especially the golf courses on the east coast dunes between St Andrews, Aberdeen and Peterhead are scenic highlights.

> **See the sky turn turquoise and pink**

The area north of the Great Glen geological fault line and 'the Highlands capital' Fort William may come across as deserted. Yet the expansive heath lands, which are a sight to behold in the autumn, are by no means a wilderness – even if Scotland tends to come across as quintessentially untamed here. The grasslands were once covered in a rustling forests and woodland. In the 19th century the wood-

land was cleared by large landowners who drove off the local crofters so that they could start large-scale sheep farms and go hunting. Today you can see the red deer that they introduced for the hunt at the places such as the Cairngorm National Park. With no natural predators – the last Scottish wolf died well more than 260 years ago – the deer population continues to expand. A mere one per cent of the original pine forests remain today.

Travelling even further north you will reach the remote Orkney and Shetland Islands both with a distinctly different, more autonomous feel to them. Their stone circles and geographical names bear testimony to the existence of settlements almost 5000 years ago and Viking connections.

1746
The last Scottish uprising, led by the Stuart Bonnie Prince Charlie, fails at the bloody Battle of Culloden

1782–1854
During the Highland Clearances, large landowners completely displaced the population of the Scottish Highlands and introduced sheep farming. By the end of the evictions the Scottish clan system had been destroyed and Gaelic largely died out as a language in Scotland

1970
Orkney and Shetland became North Sea oil powers

The islands are very accessible by car if you don't mind the ferry crossing. If you travel west you get the Celtic Hebrides. A boat trip takes visitors to the dramatic mountains of the Inner Hebrides on the isles of Jura, Mull or Skye. If

> **The aurora borealis light show**

you set course for the Outer Hebrides you will come across the other-worldly islands of North Uist, South Uist, and Harris – with its distinctive mountains and deserted beaches – and Lewis which has Britain's second-largest stone circle. These outlying islands are rather special and ideal for Scotland enthusiasts. They come here for the unique ambiance created by the Northern Lights, the psychedelic play of light of the skies on a harshly beautiful landscape.

Scotland leaves the most lasting impression when you take the time to wander off for walks into its pristine nature, be it along the coast or to the many ruins and castles. Always keep your hiking boots close at hand in your car when you travel through Britain's north.

Sandwood Bay on the edge of the Scottish Highlands: one of the country's many isolated beaches

1999
For the first time since 1707 there is a Scottish Parliament and the Labour Party won the first elections

2002
Loch Lomond and Trossachs National Park became Scotland's first national park

2009
20 years after the bombing of a Pan Am flight over Lockerbie the courts pardon the only person convicted

2014
Glasgow hosts the Commonwealth Games with participants from more than 70 nations competing in games such as cricket, lawn bowls and rugby

WHAT'S HOT

1 Beyond the kilt

Made in Scotland Fashion from the region such as designs by *Holly Fulton* is all the rage *(www.hollyfulton.com)*. You will find her creations at *Godiva (9 West Port, Edinburgh)*, a concept store with a Scottish twist. Old meets new in *Joyce Paton's* accessories *(8 East Terrace, Edinburgh)*. Once a year the *Scottish Fashion Awards* showcase the latest trends *(Glasgow Science Centre, 50 Pacific Quay, Glasgow, www.scottishfashionawards. com, photo)*.

Sphereing 2

Spin cycle Ever wondered what the spin cycle of a load of laundry feels like? To find out all you have to do is roll downhill inside a massive inflated ball! Available from *Nae Limits* in Perthshire from April to October *(Ballinluig, www.naelimits.co.uk, photo); Great Away Days (Bachilton House, Methven, Perth, www.great awaydays.co.uk);* and *House of Mulben* will send you down the hill in their Mountain Ball *(Keith, Moray, www. houseofmulben.com)*.

3 Tradition with a twist

Dance the Céilidh Thanks to modern influences the traditional *céilidh* (pronounced kay-lee) is being spiced up with bass and beats and is making inroads into nightclubs. On a Saturday you can enjoy this social dance at *The Skipinnish Ceilidh House (34–38 George Street, Oban, www.skipinnishceilidh house.com)* where traditional instruments are still used but disco lights spur on the dancers. *Hud yer Wheesht* lends Gaelic music a funky element *(www.hudyerwheesht.co.uk, photo)*. The scene's big event is the annual Battle of the Bands on the Isle of Bute *(www. scottishdance.net/music/WorldCeilidh BandComp.html)*.

The VW camper

4

Back to the future They have virtually disappeared elsewhere, however in Scotland VW camper vans are undergoing a revival. Old VW buses have been restored in recent years and now populate Scottish campsites. The Scots love the T2 series and have fans clubs that swap restoration tips on how to keep them going for as long as possible. Hire one from *Escape Campers (Eyvoll Cottage, Stepends Road, Lochwinnoch, www.escape campers.co.uk)* or from *Scotland by Camper (9 Rhannan Road, Cathcart, Glasgow, www.scotlandbycamper. com, photo)*. To accommodate camper vans and motor homes, Scotland has even introduced a special island hopping *Vehicle Island Hopscotch Ticket.* Valid for a month of island to island ferry crossings with camper van included *(www. calmac.co.uk)*.

Gyms go green

5

Fitness in nature The Scots not only want to protect their environment, they also want to keep in shape and *Green Gyms* have sprung up across the country to make this possible. The work outs give people a chance to do their bit for the environment while getting fit outside in the open air. The activities include tree planting, raking and weeding, to moving stones and rocks or transforming a tree trunk into a bench. The perfect way to keep fit and have a clear conscience! There are Green Gyms in towns wherever you go i.e. Aberdeen *(Foucausie, Grandhome, www2.btcv.org.uk, photo)* and west of Glasgow *(Ferguslie Sports Centre, 100 Blackstoun Road, Paisley)*, or picturesque locations near Inverness *(30 Millbank Road, Munlochy)*.

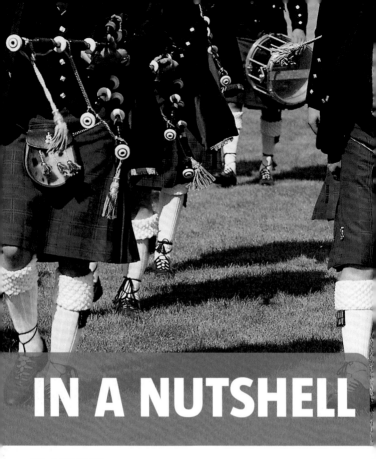

IN A NUTSHELL

BAGPIPES

The stirring and strident skirl of the bagpipe has also been used as a weapon of war: inspiring the troops and unsettling the enemy. The Romans marched to it, the English had it before the Scots (possibly introduced by the Romans) and today even the Jordanian army has adopted them. The history of the bagpipe saw its turning point in the gruesome Battle of Culloden where 100 Scottish pipers were drawn and quartered.

Despite the fact that England then outlawed the bagpipe the Scottish persevered and retained their stronghold over it to this day in much the same ingenious way they have succeeded in marketing Scotland's myths and legend.

CLANS

The term clan (*clann* in Gaelic) means a closely-knit group of inter-related families. Mac is the word for son in Scottish Gaelic. These old family tie terms are anything but dated and obsolete, on the contrary every year thousands of Americans or people residing in the South Pacific come to Scotland to peruse the country's archives for their family history, bearing testimony to the fact that the clan remains alive and well! Those in search of their ancestry have to go far back into the annals

Photo: Bagpipers at the Cowal Highland Games in Dunoon

Folklore and modernity: the Scots make the balancing act between old and new seem effortless

of history to find anything – a parliamentary decision in 1745 banned the clan system in Scotland. With this the curtain fell on a medieval social fabric that divided the Scottish identity into roughly four points of the compass. The main tribes were: the Picts from the north, the Normans from England, the Scots from Ireland and the Britains from Wales. The head of the clan had full jurisdiction over the land and lives of his clan members – leading to fierce fighting within the clans. Countless ballads also bear testimony to the fact that the clans did not like one another by any stretch of the imagination, for instance the Glen Coe massacre. Nevertheless the clans survived, at least by name. There are around five million MacDonalds (also: Macdonald, McDonald) worldwide arguably making it the most globally famous clan.

CURRENCY

The British pound is legal tender in Scotland; however you cannot pay for your purchases with the Scottish pound in the rest of the United Kingdom. Although it ought to be legal tender as there also several private banks in the United Kingdom that are permitted to issue their own notes – but no coins. These notes are official throughout the United Kingdom but are mostly only accepted where the issuing financial institution has its headquarters. The Scottish pound is printed by several institutions and therefore the images on the notes can differ for the 5, 10, 20, 50 and 100 pound notes. The Royal Bank of Scotland additionally brings out notes to the value of 1 pound. Featured on Scottish currency are the poet Robert Burns, the Firth of Forth Bridge, whisky and Orkney's Stone Age treasures.

FILM SETS

For many people their discovery of Scotland began in the cinema with the Highlands being used again and again as the backdrop to large film productions. Starting this trend in 1985 was the cult film 'Highlander' with Christopher Lambert in the leading role. The story of the immortal hero Connor MacLeod was filmed at Eilean Donan Castle among others. The massive castle set against a breathtaking backdrop of mountains also served as the setting for films such as 'Braveheart' and 'Rob Roy'. Even the more isolated untamed mountain valleys of Glen Nevis and Glencoe are a common sight on screen. It is here that Mel Gibson as Braveheart fought the English, while the opening scenes of 'Rob Roy' were filmed in the mountains above Kinlochleven near Glencoe. Scotland also served as the setting for the Harry Potter series of films: the Hogwart Express steam train en route to the magic school made its way via the stunning and picturesque Glenfinnan Viaduct that gently curves above the Glenfinnan valley on the line from Fort William to Mallaig.

'Highlander' was filmed on location at Eilean Donan Castle

FOOTBALL

In Scotland football is more than just a game of 22 men and their ball – many follow it religiously especially in Glasgow. The championship trophy goes back and forth between Celtic – the team founded by Irish Catholic immigrants – and Rangers who are largely Protestant. If you happen to wander through Glasgow East, a poorer part of the city, you ought to drop in at one of the pubs signposted with a green Celtic banner. In all probability the video showing Celtic Glasgow's defeat of Inter Milan in the European Cup of 1967 will be on the screen as you step inside. See *www.rangers.co.uk* or *www.celticfc.co.uk*.

GAELIC

'Slàinte' is how the people living on the Hebrides, the Highlands and Glasgow drink a toast. The word is Gaelic – the old Celtic language that has survived in several corners of Scotland to this day. Especially the Outer Hebrides and the west coast of the Highlands have pockets

where Gaelic is still spoken and understood. Even the road signs on the western islands are bilingual, there are also Gaelic radio and television broadcasts and Gaelic language lessons in the schools. Approximately one per cent of the Scottish people are fluent in the old language.

GOING GREEN

The Scottish National Party's grasp of power with Alex Salmond as First Minister (Prime Minister) seems to have heralded in an ecological era in Scotland. There have been signs of increasing environmental consciousness and a heavy drive to the expansion of renewable energies. Europe's largest wind farm is 15km/9mi from Glasgow and supplies electricity to 180,000 households and there are also investments being made in offshore energy and wave power. It is Scotland's ambitious goal that renewable energies make up 80 per cent of the country's electricity needs by 2020. As a visitor to the country this wave of environmental consciousness is however not that apparent as yet. Many hotels and guest houses still have old sash windows instead of double glazing and the cholesterol-rich Scottish breakfast is a far cry from organic and healthy nutrition. Even so, the environmentally conscious age is increasingly making inroads into tourism and the oval green sign with the wording *Green Tourism* is often seen in the entrances to accommodation, tourist attractions, restaurants and public buildings. Businesses throughout the United Kingdom are awarded the green label for sustainable and ecological management. See *www.green-business.co.uk*

HIGHLANDS

Homecoming in the Highlands: after an absence of 1000 years the elk is making its return. They were eradicated by people and now a Scotsman has made it his mis-

Kilted and muscle-bound – a typical Games participant

sion to reverse this intervention in nature. He is multi-millionaire Paul Lister, owner of the Alladale estate north of Inverness. Lister wants to return Scottish fauna and flora to its original state on his 25,000 acre private estate. Its barren mountain ridges were once densely forested with Scots pine, oak and birch and woodland. Wild boar roamed here as did wolves, bears and elks. It all came to an end when profit hungry sheep farmers claimed the land. They expelled the local subsistence farmers and cut down the forests. They cultivated pastures for their sheep and introduced red deer for their hunts. The face of the Highlands and the islands was forever changed. In the interim only the red deer remain, some 500,000 of them roam the moors today. It is Paul Lister's dream to turn back time. He has taken advice from scientists and has planted hundreds of thousands of the old Scots pines and has imported elk from Sweden and has also converted abandoned farm-houses into lodges for visitors to the Highlands *(see p. 69)*. He organises deer hunts in the name of ecological renewal until the day when wolves and bears will call the Highlands their home once more. See www.alladale.com

HIGHLANDS GAMES

● Centuries ago when the king was in search of new bodyguards, or when clan chiefs met, they held a kind of Olympiad for strong men: the Highland Games. These are still held today, 100 throughout Scotland showcasing more than 40 disciplines. *Tossing the caber* is when kilted muscle men throw a tree trunk and get it to somersault a few times. *Throwing the hammer* is a heavy metal ball attached to a cane handle while *putting the stone* is similar to shot put although it is more light-footed and performed to a curious Highlands tap dance. The Games of course are also where the best bagpipe players can be heard. The most famous take place in Braemar at the beginning of September under the auspices of the Queen.

INNOVATORS

Bacteriologist Alexander Fleming (born in 1881) discovered penicillin after extensive research which earned him the Nobel Prize for Medicine. Scotland has produced not only physicians and researchers: Charles Mackintosh (1766–1843) developed waterproof clothing and to this day the raincoat retains his name; John Dunlop (1840–1921) invented air-filled tyres; the steam machine goes back to James Watt (1736–1819) and Alexander Graham Bell (1847–1922) was the father of the telephone. There is to be an explanation for why such a small country has been so blessed with such genius. In 1546 the reformer John Knox insisted on compulsory schooling. Scotland's high academic standard has been maintained to this day – be it innovations in the field of micro-electronics in the Silicon Glen or in scientific tests to manipulate genetic material – here Dolly the cloned sheep springs to mind, she was the result of pioneering work done in Roslin.

LITERATURE

Scottish literature is dominated by an impressive triumvirate: Sir Walter Scott, Robert Louis Stevenson and Robert Burns. Burns (1759–96), poet of the pubs and drinking holes, is Scotland's national poet and on 25 January the Scottish eat haggis – a sheep's stomach stuffed with innards – in his honour. 'Ode to a Haggis' is his famous tribute to this dish made famous by him throughout Scotland. Sir Walter Scott's (1771–1832) legacy continues in his romantic novels while Robert Louis Stevenson's (1850-94) 'Treasure Island' among other novels has secured him a place in bookshelves worldwide. A popular 20th century author is Alasdair Gray who occasionally also illustrates his works himself. But none can beat the astronomical sales figures of J. K. Rowling for her bestselling Harry Potter books.

MUSIC

Contemporary Scotland is also known for its melodious rock and the popular band Franz Ferdinand from Glasgow (which has absolutely nothing to do with the Habsburg Archduke) is a great example of the phenomenon. This indie Scottish rock band seem to have a very similar beginnings to that of some other Scottish bands i.e. a combination of study at the Glasgow School of Art and believe it or not, a drunken brawl. Their success has inspired other bands from the heart of the country such as Belle & Sebastian, Travis, Delgado, Mogwai and Amy MacDonald – their unique indie sounds are melancholic at times but always distinctly Scottish in tone.

TARTANS AND KILTS

The Gaelic word *tartan* means a check patterned wool fabric which is used for *kilts*, a word which is Scandinavian in origin. To make the skirt-like kilt a length of tartan (6–8yds) is pleated and wrapped around the waist, the family clan determines the tartan, the chilly weather calls for knee high socks, while a small knife in the sock ensures that small repairs can be conducted. Kilts were once the perfect outfit for the poor inhabitants of the marshy Highlands but after the Battle of Culloden in 1746 kilts were banned. Offenders of the new Dress Act decree faced imprisonment and even banishment. In 1782 the ban was lifted and the kilt allowed but by then the old patterns had long been forgotten. Today the kilt is worn primarily at ceremonies and weddings. Ask a Scotsman what he is wearing under his kilt and he may do a cartwheel to satisfy your curiosity!

FOOD & DRINK

The Scottish start their day with a hearty cooked breakfast that can include kippers, smoked herring or haddock. Also on the breakfast menu are oat porridge and oatcakes – a savoury oat biscuit cooked on the griddle or baked – and Orkney is renowned for the best!

Today hotel guests can eschew the Scottish breakfast and choose the continental breakfast instead. Many B&Bs nowadays also serve this lighter breakfast option.

In comparison to breakfast, Scottish lunch tends to be a light snack such as a sandwich or homemade soup at the pub or your proverbial fish and chips wrapped in a newspaper.

Scottish high tea is a traditional culinary delight served between 4pm and 5pm in the afternoon and plays itself out as an opulent unhurried feast not to be missed. This is not a cup of Green tea and a biscuit, but rather the finest in Ceylon teas accompanied by an array of mouth-watering sandwiches and pastries and freshly baked scones served with jam and cream. If you meet up for dinner later on (from about 7pm) expect only the finest of the island's produce as Scotland's cuisine is experiencing a new lease on life.

For years Scottish cuisine had to contend with a poor reputation. If the truth be told, lots of locals still indulge in the mighty

Photo: Raisin scones served with whipped cream and blueberries

Far better than its reputation: Scottish cuisine entices with its delicate scallops and delicious shortbread

Scottish breakfast without giving their health a second thought. However, a growth in Scotland's economy, and flourishing tourism in the cities, has ensured the expansion of the country's culinary repertoire. In Glasgow and Edinburgh you'll find the whole spectrum of restaurants from sushi to Mexican (and of course vegetarian) and the wealthy middle class have also embraced healthy Mediterranean cuisine. Chic Italian restaurants are guaranteed to be bursting at the seams at night and in the cities there are countless delis selling Scottish salmon alongside Parma ham and balsamic vinegar. Traditional fish and chips shops are still around but they are usually found in the smaller towns. So what is typical Scottish cuisine? However you define it, one thing is certain: it has changed for the better. The reason

LOCAL SPECIALITIES

▶ **Arbroath smokies** – smoked haddock served warm, named after a fishing village on the east coast

▶ **Atholl brose** – the ingredients of this punch include oatmeal brose, honey, whisky and cream, traditionally served on New Year's Eve

▶ **Black pudding** – the famous blood and oat sausage comes from Stornoway in the Outer Hebrides

▶ **Cairnsmore** – a nutty hard cheese made from sheep's milk, the perfect end to a meal

▶ **Cock-a-leekie** – a hearty chicken and leek soup popular at the coast and on the islands

▶ **Cranachan** – a delectable dessert of fresh raspberries, honey and whipped cream served in a glass with a dash of whisky for good measure

▶ **Cullen skink** – a hearty, creamy soup of smoked haddock, onion, milk and potato

▶ **Deep-fried Mars bar** – ice cold Mars bar dipped in batter and fried, not an urban myth!

▶ **Haggis** – Scotland's national dish has gained international fame thanks to Robert Burns. Offal minced with onion, bread, spices, eggs and flour encased in a sheep's stomach and left to simmer. Although opinions may vary it is worth a try in a good restaurant (photos)

▶ **Hotchpotch** – a hearty lamb and mixed vegetable stew, popular in the Borders region

▶ **Roastit Bubbly-Jock** – Christmas turkey traditionally stuffed with oysters and chestnuts

▶ **Skirlie** –dish made with oatmeal fried with onion and seasoning

▶ **Stovies** – this dish owes its name to the stove on which it is cooked. It is a lamb or beef potato stew that is perfect for a cold day and best served with a glass of ice cold buttermilk

for this is the return to high-grade locally grown produce. Top chef Claire MacDonald has been instrumental in generating greater creativity in the kitchen not only on her television programme but with her popular cookbooks. Long before other chefs endorsed local produce she promoted the use of wild mushrooms from the forests in Kingussie and beef from the Highlands and championed local cattle breeds such as Aberdeen-Angus, Galloway, Longhorn, Shorthorn and Highland.

Regional produce has been the key to the renaissance in Scotland's upscale restaurant cuisine. Scotland now has 16 Michelin stars that attest to the high quality of its restaurants – four of these have been awarded to restaurants in Edinburgh. The sought-after ranking has even gone to some small country hotels in remote regions such as *The Peat Inn* in the centre of the Fife peninsula *(closed Mon | tel. 01334 84 02 06 | Expensive)* or *The Albannach* in Lochinver → *p. 84*, the *Knockinaam Lodge* near Stranrear *(daily | 01776 81 04 71 | www.knockinaamlodge.com | Expensive)* and Claire MacDonald's *Kinloch Lodge* on Skye *(daily | Sleat | tel. 01471 83 33 33 | Expensive)* where Brazilian Marcello Tully is the head chef. The combination of nature, romantic fireplaces and Michelin-star cuisine makes Scotland a very attractive destination even in the winter when it is worth looking out for special package deals. Gourmet cuisine has also left its mark on some of the more rural pubs and, by all accounts, on eating out in the cities. Daily specials with two or three course menus are great value for money. Fresh fish is a sought-after speciality of

Scottish cuisine. On a trip along the east coast you will come across small towns like Arbroath where the smell of burning charcoal and sea salt lingers in the air. Fishing boats are anchored in the harbour and lobster traps can be seen all along the pier. The smokehouses produce smoked halibut and salmon – freshly caught and cured – that is absolutely delicious! However, most chefs prefer fish from the cleaner west coast where the lobsters and shellfish are of a higher quality.

Despite its vast culinary repertoire there is one thing that is missing in Scotland: a good glass of wine. Cellar masters have to order in from Italy, Spain, South Africa, California and of course France – it's a fact that Leith (Edinburgh's port) is the destination for some of the finest Bordeaux. As wine is best served with cheese it should naturally be one of Scotland's own. Try the *Lanark Blue*, which looks like Gorgonzola, it is made from sheep's milk from the Borders region and is creamy white with blue veining. Also highly commended is the *White Diamond* from the Galloway region, a delicate and mild cream cheese that goes perfectly with strawberries.

A feast for the senses: whisky has 800 aromas

SHOPPING

Whatever keepsakes you choose to take back home, only the best will do. Avoid buying a kilt made of acrylic or a blend, a jumper that shrinks after the first wash or cheap booze that dares to call itself whisky. Instead, buy these items where they are produced – from Scotland's genuine craftsmen, weavers and distilleries.

CASHMERE

Scotland is well known for its top quality light-weight cashmere knitwear such as cardigans and vests and prices are good as the wool is imported on a large scale. You need look no further than *Johnstons of Elgin* which is said to have the best quality and you can buy directly on location (*Visitor Centre | New Mill, Elgin | Mon–Thu 10am–4pm | www.johnstonsofelgin.com*).

DESIGN

You will find poetic and surreal textiles, lampshades and wallpaper at designers INSIDER TIP ▸ *Timorous Beasties* – the shop's name is taken from a Robert Burns poem – the creative team studied at the Glasgow School of Art and their Glasgow store is at *384 Great Western Road (www.timorous beasties.com).* In Edinburgh you will come across a varied and witty selection of young Scottish designers at the *Concrete Wardrobes* cooperative (*50 A Broughton Street | www.concretewardrobe.co.uk*).

KILTS

The kilt is actually a very comfortable piece of clothing and it is fast catching on among Scotland's younger generation with many following tradition and wearing it for weddings and festivals. The kilt is also experiencing a revival in the cities, albeit with some less traditional versions, such as those made from black leather, silk or even PVC. You will find amazing kilts – both traditional or completely over the top – at *Howard Nickelby's* shop on the Royal Mile. *21st Century Kilts | 61 High St, Edinburgh | tel. 0131 5 57 02 56 | www.21stcenturykilts.com*

TWEED

Only sheep's wool spun on the Outer Hebrides and handwoven in cottage in-

The kilt is iconic and no shopping list should be without this essential souvenir of your Scotland trip

dustries on the islands can carry the *Harris Tweed* label. The local *Harris Tweed Authority* certifies and monitors its production. The resilient cloth with its herringbone pattern has been produced on the islands of Harris and Lewis for centuries. Edinburgh's drapers then turn it into coats and waistcoats and other garments.

Harris Tweed has once again become a fashionable textile: the weaver Donald John Mackay, from the coastal village of Luskentyre on Harris, made headlines recently when Nike purchased miles of material from him for the manufacture of a retro sports shoe. The traditional colours for the wool need not be upheld today and the weavers in the tiny houses on Harris who sell their wool on Lewis don't have to keep to the traditional patterns and will happily reach deep into their colour repertoire to satisfy customers from outside Scotland.

WHISKY

And then there is the whisky! Whisky is unique to the region it is produced in because each distillery uses water from local creeks. There are three distilleries that stand out: for the most exciting distillery tour try *Highland Park Distillery* in Kirkwall on Orkney – here barley is still laid out in the cellar using the floor malting process. The charming *Edradour* at Pitlochry is the smallest distillery in Scotland and it produces a variety of single malts as well as a blended whisky, the *House of Lords*. For whisky with a peaty taste then a trip to the Isle of Islays *Lagavulin, Laphroaig, Ardbeg* and *Coal Isla* distilleries is a must. Their coastal location and the tour guides' fascinating anecdotes will make shopping for a choice whisky effortless *(www.highlandpark.co.uk, www.edradour.co.uk, www.islaywhiskysociety.com)*.

THE PERFECT ROUTE

THE SOUTH: EVOCATIVE AND MYSTICAL

Make a beeline from ① *Edinburgh* → p. 52 inland and let the evocative south unfold before you. First stop: the mysterious Rosslyn Chapel. Now head on to the heart and soul of the Borders region where the picturesque little towns of Peebles, Galashiels, Melrose and Kelso lie alongside the River Tweed. Here is also where you'll find Sir Walter Scott's home, Abbotsford and several abbey ruins are located at short intervals from one another. Not to be missed is Dryburgh Abbey. To get to Dumfries it is best to take the ② *A 708* → p. 35 scenic route. Pack sandwiches so you can picnic en route alongside the lake.

A WEALTH OF EXPERIENCES: CITY, COUNTRY, FERRY

The drive from Dumfries along the south coast to Stranaer takes you to the ③ *Scottish Riviera* → p. 41 home to the thriving Logan Botanic Gardens made possible by the Gulf Stream. Carry on along the sea in the direction of Ayr, past lighthouses and fortresses and you will find yourself on the best route to the hustle and bustle (photo left) of ④ *Glasgow* → p. 42. If you are ready to visit your first island, then take the ferry across to ⑤ *Arran* → p. 49 at Ardrossan.

ISLAND HOPPING: CLEAR YOUR HEAD

Arran is the springboard to the remote Kintyre Peninsula and the picture-perfect beach at Machrihanish. Continue your island hop to ⑥ *Islay* → p. 83 then on to Jura and enjoy whisky tours on both islands. The ferry crossing from Islay (photo right) to ⑦ *Oban* → p. 82 will blow away the cobwebs and clear your head.

THE HEBRIDES: SCENIC CRUISE

In Oban you can once again board another boat – this time to cruise through the Sound of Mull – a narrow strip of ocean between the mainland and the green and mountainous isle of ⑧ *Mull* → p. 83 which is home to numerous species of birds of prey. Then carry on to the Outer Hebrides.

BEN NEVIS: SET YOUR SIGHTS HIGH

Equally exciting is driving through the western Highlands with its mountainous landscape to ⑨ *Fort William* → p. 66. Here you can climb Ben Nevis, Scotland's highest mountain. Alternatively make a short pit stop of it then continue your journey

Experience the diverse facets of Scotland on an extended roundtrip with detours to a dream beach and to the Highlands

along the west coast to ⑩ *Skye* → p. 80 the most diverse of the Hebridean islands. There are two options to get there: coastward to Arisaig and Mallaig – from where pleasure boats set off to the Small Isles and a ferry takes you to Armadale on southern Skye – or the other option is to travel to Eilean Donan Castle and cross the bridge on to the island from there.

LONELY AND REMOTE

The route from Skye to ⑪ *Ullapool* → p. 84 is quite a lonely one. Accompanied by the peat moors the road north takes you through dramatic landscapes of lakes and solitary, high mountain peaks. Scrabster at Thurso is where the car ferry sets off for the archaeological paradise of ⑫ *Orkney* → p. 86.

ALONG THE COAST

From the cape there are hours of driving along the scenic coast south to ⑬ *Inverness* → p. 68. If you decide to travel via Dornoch Firth instead of taking the bridge, you should stop off at the Alladale estate at Ardgay for a guided tour of the reforested Highlands.

A ROYAL VISIT

From Inverness your journey takes you through quaint villages nestled along the coast. At ⑭ *Aberdeen* → p. 62 follow the path of the River Dee – the forested route will take you past Balmoral, the Scottish royal palace. Edinburgh is close but an excursion to the delightful coastal towns of the ⑮ *Fife peninsula* → p. 73 is a must. After your detour you will cross the Firth of Forth Bridge and head to Edinburgh.

1800km/1118 mi. Driving time: 31 hours. Detailed map of the route on the back cover, in the road atlas and the pull-out map.

THE SOUTH

Newcastle upon Tyne in northern England is where the Roman border begins in the form of Hadrian's Wall which ends in Carlisle in the north-west of England. The wall was to prevent incursions by the Picts and the Scots from present day Scotland. Fortress ruins like *Caerlaverock Castle* at Dumfries are evidence of the battles between the English and the Scots some 1000 years later, as are strongholds like *Smailholm Tower* in the hilly Lowlands or Southern Uplands – another name for the area from Edinburgh to Glasgow. Compared to the deserted Highlands, the Lowlands are characterised by beautiful small towns such as Melrose, Jedburgh and Kelso where romantic abbey ruins are a reminder of Scotland's Catholic past. The area's country roads are popular with cyclists and the coastal footpath, the *Southern Uplands Way*, attracts ramblers and hikers. The Lowlands are in the western region of Dumfries and Galloway with the Borders region to the east. In the west you can walk in the footsteps of the national poet, Robert Burns. In Galloway the coastal section, tempered by the mild Gulf Stream climate, is well worth a visit, especially the *Galloway Forest Park*. The Borders is also where you will find Sir Walter Scott's home, *Abbotsford* where he created the novels that brought him worldwide acclaim.

Photo: Culzean Castle

Romantic Lowlands: stay on the trail of Scotland's famous poets and explore castles and ancient abbeys

BORDERS REGION

In south-east of Scotland, a lush green landscape of rolling hills stretches out between Edinburgh, Moffat and the English border, one that has both great scenic beauty and a turbulent history.

Fly fishing is a common sight here on rivers such as the Tweed, Esk, Teviot and Ettrick. The romantic sight of Early Gothic abbey ruins, dream castles and fortified towers in and around small towns like Melrose, Jedburgh, Kelso, Selkirk and Peebles are a delightful contrast to natural wonders you can hike to, such as the *Grey Mare's Tail* waterfall and the exhilarating coastal cliffs of *St Abb's Head*. It was the charming

Borders region scenery, and the history of bitter border wars fought with England in the late Middle Ages, that formed the backdrop of Sir Walter Scott's historical novels. To this day tourism to Scotland, turned into an opera by Donizetti), 'The Heart of Midlothian' and 'Waverley'. His urge to write may also stem from a mountain of debt. Collectors' items still showcased in Abbotsford House today include

Sir Walter Scott's desk in Abbotsford House: just as he left it

Hollywood epics and the opera benefit from his works.

SIGHTSEEING

ABBOTSFORD HOUSE ★
(123 E3) (*∅ L14*)

In 1812 novelist Sir Walter Scott (1771–1832) acquired the estate on the River Tweed and built his Victorian-style dream castle with countless turrets and bay windows. Visitors can view the desk at which he wrote the more than 40 novels that captivated the imagination of readers worldwide. Integral to his subject matter is Scottish folklore seen in many of his works such as 'Lucia of Lammermuir' (which was the sword of freedom fighter Rob Roy, the chalice Bonnie Prince Charlie drank from and countless other memorabilia from Scotland's rich history. On his visit, the German late 19th century author Theodor Fontane expressed his contempt for Sir Walter's hoarding. But it is precisely the authenticity of the novelist's Scottish abode that has made it a draw card with tourists from around the world who come to see Scott's world, where he may literally have written himself to ill health. His favourite spot is in the nearby Eildon Hills and is now known as ☆ *Scott's View. 4km/2.4mi south-east of Galashiels | March–Oct daily 9.30am–5pm | £8 | www.scotts abbotsford.co.uk*

A 708 ⭐

(122–123 C–D 3–4) (*ⓂK–L14*)

A dream road: if you take the A 708 from Moffat towards Galashiels and to the Border abbeys, you may think that you are already in the middle of the Highlands. The scenery surrounding the *Grey Mare's Tail* waterfall is by far the most mountainous and the hike up to the waterfall source in Loch Skeen is well worth it. After the steep climb you can enjoy a **INSIDER TIP** romantic picnic and a swim. The view on the 🔻 way down is spectacular. Carry on driving 8km/5mi to *Tibbie Shiel's Inn (St Mary's Loch | Budget)*, the perfect stop for a cup of coffee. Even the authors Sir Walter Scott and James Hogg (1770–1835) came to relax and chat and Hogg's statue overlooks the delightful *St Mary's Loch*.

DRYBURGH ABBEY

(123 E3) (*Ⓜ M14*)

Sir Walter Scott was laid to rest here beneath mighty cedars in 1832. The most romantic among the Borders abbeys is an early Gothic Premonstratensian abbey dating back to 1150 located alongside the River Tweed. *8km/5mi south-east of Melrose | same opening times and website as Jedburgh Abbey | £5.50*

INSIDER TIP HERMITAGE CASTLE

(123 D4) (*Ⓜ L15*)

The lonely landscape of the surrounding area makes the mighty ramparts of this partly derelict fortress from the 13th century look even more imposing. Standing beneath them it is easy to visualise the bitter border wars fought here or a sombre scene from a Shakespeare play. Mary Queen of Scots rode all the way here in 1566 to take care of her beloved Bothwell, a feat that almost killed her. *10km/6.2mi south of Hawick | April–Sept daily 9.30am–5.30pm | £4 | www.historic-scotland.gov.uk*

JEDBURGH ABBEY ⭐

(123 E3–4) (*Ⓜ M14*)

The best preserved and most impressive abbey ruin of the four great Borders' abbeys. Augustinian monks have led a monastic life here since the 12th century. An audio-visual account and excavation pieces transport you back in time. *Jedburgh | April–Sept daily 9.30am–17.30pm, Oct–March daily 9.30am–4.30pm, Sun 2pm–4.30pm | £5.50 | www.historic-scotland.gov.uk*

THE JIM CLARK ROOM

(123 E2) (*Ⓜ M13*)

Trophies, photographs and souvenirs pay tribute to the two-time Scottish Formula 1

MARCO POLO HIGHLIGHTS

champion who died on the Hockenheim racing track in 1968. *March–Sept Mon–Sat 10.30am–1pm, 2pm–4.30pm, Sun 2pm–4pm | admission free | 44 Newtown Street | Duns*

MELROSE
(123 D–E3) (*ⅅ L14*)

The ruins of the abbey, that King David I had built for the French Cistercians in 1136, are in the most beautiful Borders village. The abbey was built with a special resting place for what was believed to be the heart of Scotland's national hero, Robert the Bruce. A 9 km/5.5mi trail from the town takes hikers to the surrounding ☀ *Eildon Hills* with their breathtaking views of the River Tweed and the abbey. *April–Sept daily 9.30am–6.30pm, Oct–March Mon–Sat 9.30am–4.30pm | £5.50*

SMAILHOLM TOWER (123 E3) (*ⅅ M14*)

This is an excellent example of a 15th century fortified Borders residential tower. Visible for miles, it stands on a dramatic crag as a reminder of the Border Wars. Today it houses a tapestries and costumes exhibition. *April–Sept daily 9.30am–5.30pm, Oct Mon–Wed, Sat/Sun 9.30am–4.30pm, Nov to March Sat/Sun 9.30am–4.30pm | £4.50 | 9km/5.5mi west of Kelso*

ST ABB'S HEAD ★ (123 F2) (*ⅅ N13*)

Here the east coast is at its dramatic best, the grassy slopes and cliffs are home to thousands of seabirds. It is one of Scotland's most beautiful coastal wildlife reserves (butterflies galore!) and is especially captivating in the early morning mist or at twilight. Stay over in Eyemouth or in Coldingham. *10km/6.2mi north of Eyemouth*

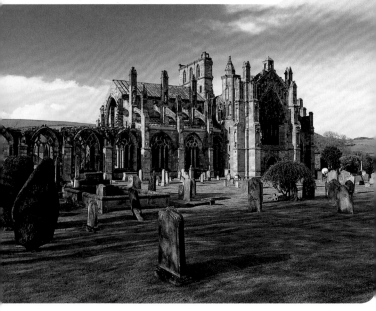

Melrose Abbey: where Scottish kings were laid to rest beneath Gothic arches

TRAQUAIR HOUSE ⭐
(123 D3) *(ØJ L13)*

Originally a hunting lodge, this cosy country house and beautiful park dates back to 1107. It has been home to the Jacobite Catholic Maxwell-Stuart family for centuries and Mary, Queen of Scots, also spent the night. Some of the memorabilia accumulated over the years is on display – in some parts fascinating and in others rather kitsch. End your excursion with a glass of house ale in the inviting beer garden. *April–Sept daily noon–5pm, Jun–Aug from 10.30am, Oct/Nov daily 11am–4pm | £7.50 | www.traquair.co.uk | Innerleithen*

FOOD & DRINK

MARMION'S (123 D–E3) *(ØJ L14)*
A relaxed bistro opposite Melrose Abbey that serves tasty light meals, the salads are especially recommended. *Closed Sun | Buccleuch Street, Melrose | tel. 01896 82 22 45 | Moderate*

SPORTS & ACTIVITIES

INSIDER TIP **TWEEDHOPE SHEEPDOGS** ● (123 D3) *(ØJ L14)*
As far as Viv Billingham is concerned Border collies are not pets. The charismatic author and dog breeder – a local celebrity in her own right thanks to some TV appearances – offers collie dog demonstrations at the idyllic St Mary's Loch. With a series of commands and whistles her dogs to keep a herd of sheep in check, making the demonstration seem like a finely orchestrated ballet. She also entertains with interesting accounts of how herds used to be driven across hundreds of miles to the marketplace. *St Mary's Loch | by appointment only | £5 | tel. 01750 4 22 48 | www.stockdogsavvy.wordpress. com/2010/03/02/viv-billingham*

WHERE TO STAY

CASTLE VENLAW (123 D3) *(ØJ L13)*
This hotel is a 250 year old castle with a tower and offers suites with four-poster beds and a cosy bar. Very romantic and therefore a favourite among couples on honeymoon. *Edinburgh Road, Peebles | tel. 01721 72 03 84 | www.venlaw.co.uk | Expensive*

CHURCHES HOTEL AND RESTAURANT
(123 E3) *(ØJ N13)*
Dating back to 1790 this boutique hotel was modernised in 2000. Nestled between several churches in a fishing village on the east coast near St Abb's Head, it has individually furnished rooms and a cosy conservatory overlooking the harbour serving gourmet seafood fare *(Moderate–Expensive)*. The small hotel is also a popular wedding venue. *6 rooms | Albert Road, Eyemouth | tel. 01890 75 04 01 | www.churcheshotel.co.uk | Moderate*

EDENWATER HOUSE
(123 E3) *(ØJ M13)*
For the romantics among their guests hoteliers Jeff and Jacqui Kelly will gladly light a few extra candles. You get the feeling that this couple really enjoy the hospitality industry. INSIDER TIP Jacqui is a superb chef *(Moderate)* and the quiet atmosphere of the old vicarage with beautiful garden as well as the inviting rooms will make you want to extend your stay. There is a separate smoking lounge. *4 rooms | Bridge Street, Ednam near Kelso | tel. 01573 22 40 70 | www.edenwater house.co.uk | Moderate*

INFORMATION

There are Tourist Information Centres in all the towns mentioned: *www.visitscot- tishborders.com*

DUMFRIES

(122 B–C5) (*K15*) **The largest small town in the south-west has a population of 33,000 and has a tranquil location on the River Nith.**

Scotland's national poet, Robert Burns, spent his last years here and today you can still read some of his poems in his local haunt, the *Globe Inn.*

SIGHTSEEING

BURNS' HOUSE

Poet Robert Burns (1759–96) spent the last three years of his life in this sandstone house. The father of twelve worked as a tax collector. His wife Jean Armour lived here until 1834 so that the house really ought to have been named after her. On display is Burns' study and various memorabilia. *Burns Street | April–Sept Mon–Sat 10am–5pm, Sun 2pm–5pm, Oct–March Tue–Sat 10am–1pm and 2pm–5pm | admission free*

DUMFRIES MUSEUM ☆

The highlight of this museum is the camera obscura built into the top floor of the old windmill. In good weather you can see panoramic views of the town. *April–Sept Mon–Sat 10am–5pm, Sun 2pm–5pm | £2.50*

FOOD & DRINK

GLOBE INN

A beer and pub lunch at Robert Burns' local haunt is a must if you're a fan. But be warned: sit in his favourite chair and you will end up having to order a round of drinks for everyone in the pub! *56 High Street | tel. 01387 25 23 35 | Budget*

WHERE TO STAY

CORSEWALL LIGHTHOUSE

(121 D5) (*G16*)

This old lighthouse tower has been beaming its warning across Scotland's south-west coast for two centuries. Today it is also a hotel with well-furnished, first-rate

Traders and farmers at the Dumfries Agricultural Show

suites on the edge of a spectacular cliff. Guaranteed to be highlights of your stay: the dramatic sea views and the five-course menu served in such a unique location. *10 rooms | Stranraer | tel. 01776 85 32 20 | www.lighthousehotel.co.uk | Moderate*

CRIFFEL INN

An enchanting village pub right next to the INSIDER TIP *Sweetheart Abbey ruins*. The Criffel Mountains in the backdrop make for a picture perfect setting. *7 rooms | New Abbey (13km/8mi south of Dumfries) | tel. 01387 85 03 05 | www.criffel-inn.co.uk | Budget*

INFORMATION

DUMFRIES & GALLOWAY TOURIST BOARD

64 Whitesands | Dumfries | tel. 01387 25 38 62 | www.visitdumfriesandgalloway.co.uk

WHERE TO GO

CAERLAVEROCK CASTLE ★ ●
(122 C6) (*ω K15*)

Pure romanticism: this charming triangular fortress ruin surrounded by a moat is 13km/8mi south of Dumfries. It dates back to the medieval Border wars and has imposing ramparts (the damage to the masonry was probably done in the last siege) and a Renaissance façade was added to it in the 17th century – in the evening it makes for the perfect backdrop to a INSIDER TIP romantic picnic. Alongside it, there is a huge bird sanctuary in the marshlands of the Solway Firth that is ideal for a walk. INSIDER TIP Both are also excellent winter destinations. *Glencaple | April–Sept daily 9.30am–5.30pm, Oct–March 9.30am–4.30pm | £5.50 | www.historic-scotland.gov.uk*

CULZEAN CASTLE ⤴ (121 D3) (*ω H14*)

Perched on a cliff this manor house is located 70km/43mi north-west of Dumfries. Landscaped gardens take you into its elegant interior with impressive curved staircase. The castle and park are at their most spectacular in the evening bathed in the sunset. Some may find the 13 pound entrance fee a little steep. *April–Oct daily 10am–5.30pm | www.culzeanexperience.org*

GALLOWAY FOREST PARK
(121 E4) (*ω H15*)

Nature at its best: Great Britain's largest forest park lies near Newton Stewart. Take a hike to *Bruce's Stone* on Loch Trool which commemorates the Robert the Bruce's victory over the English in 1307. Plenty of informative material available at the *Visitor Centre* – cake and snacks also on sale. *Admission free | www.gallowayforestpark.com*

INSIDER TIP GLENKILN RESERVOIR SCULPTURES (122 B5) (*ω K15*)

There are no sign and no opening hours: Sir William Keswick's Sculpture Park is open to those that can find it. In the middle of a glen, between hill moors and sheep pastures you'll come across statues by sculptors such as Henry Moore, Jacob Epstein and Auguste Rodin. Sir William, a Scottish industrialist, had the park commissioned in the early 1950s. It surrounds Glenkiln Reservoir. The famous Henry Moore bronze 'King and Queen' is on a hillside above the lake. Be prepared to hike some distance to enjoy the works as the park stretches over nearly 4 miles. *6km/3.7mi north-west of Dumfries at Shawhead*

GRETNA GREEN (123 D6) (*ω L15*)

This small town is world famous for its Old Blacksmith's Shop where for 200 years minors could tie the knot without parental consent. Young lovers would flee to Gretna Green across the border from England to take advantage of Scotland's less rigid marriage policies. The local blacksmith was the commissioner of oaths who performed the weddings – the blacksmith forge is now a museum and Gretna Green remains a very popular wedding destination. However, today the bride and groom have to be at least 16 years old.

Knockinaam Lodge (10 rooms | Portpatrick | tel. 01776 810471 | www.knockinaam lodge.com | Expensive | 5 course menu Moderate–Expensive | reservation essential!). INSIDER TIP The bar stocks more than 150 whiskies.

LOW KIRKBRIDE FARM ☺
(122 B5) (*Ω K15*)
This is an eco-friendly cattle and sheep farm offering lovely rooms. The cattle

Love knows no bounds: and (almost) no age Gretna Green

Old Blacksmith's Shop | www.gretnagreen. org | approx. 25 km south-east of Dumfries

LOGAN BOTANIC GARDENS
(121 D6) (*Ω G16*)
Thanks to the warm Gulf Stream, tropical and subtropical plants thrive in the extreme south-west of Scotland. *(March–Oct daily 10am–5pm | £3.50)*. Aside from the magnificent gardens, another reason for the trip is the excellent country hotel

farmed here are the Belted Galloways, an old Scottish heritage breed with a distinctive white belt around their stomachs. *6 rooms | near Glenmidge, 16km/10mi north of Dumfries | tel. 01387 820258 | www.lowkirkbridefarm.com | Budget*

ROBERT BURNS BIRTHPLACE
MUSEUM (121 E3) (*Ω H14*)
Robert Burns was born in a cottage in Alloway on 25 January 1759. In 2011 a large,

new museum dedicated to the Scottish national hero and poet was opened. The museum is set in 10 acres of countryside, and constructed of wood that lets in a lot of natural light, just as Burns would have wanted. There are interactive displays, original manuscripts, 5000 items of memorabilia paying tribute to the author of *Auld Lang Syne* as well as contemporary art. *April–Sept daily 10am–5.30pm, Oct–March daily 10am–5pm | £8 | www.burns museum.org.uk*

SCOTTISH RIVIERA
(122 B–C6) (*ØJ K16*)

The A 710 coastal road from Dumfries to Castle Douglas takes you along the scenic Scottish Riviera, past placid bays, beautiful beaches and wonderful views. The oddly shaped, snow-white lighthouse of Southerness is well worth a detour. When you reach Rockcliffe you should park your car and take the mile hike along the bay to Kippford where you end up at the *Anchor Inn (tel. 01556 62 02 05 | Budget)* at the small harbour where you'll be served excellent pub food.

WIGTOWN BAY
(121 E–F6) (*ØJ J16*)

This remote tip of land is well worth a detour. The small town of *Wigtown* is Scotland's *National Book Town* – you can take your pick from four million books. In September it hosts a ten-day book festival *(www.wigtownbookfestival.com)*. Further south is the town of *Whithorn* and the *Whithorn Trust's Visitor Story Centre* where you'll find excavations dating back to the founder of Scottish Christendom: St Ninian was the Pict's apostle in the 5th century.

Not far from the *Visitor Story Centre (Easter–Oct | daily 10.30am–5pm)* is the award-winning *Ravenstone Deli (Tue–Sat)* serving local ☺ organic foods. A few

miles on is the atmospheric and elegant *Steam Packet Inn* with lovely rooms right on the bay (bookings essential!). *4 rooms | tel. 01988 50 03 34 | www.steampacket inn.biz | Budget | about 60km/37mi west of Dumfries*

LOW BUDGET

▶ *Broadmeadows Hostel*: rustic and off the beaten track at Selkirk (off the A 708), ideal for hikers and cyclists. *20 beds | Yarrowford | tel. 01750 7 62 62 | www.syha.org.uk*

▶ *Melrose Youth Hostel*: Georgian, spacious good quality accommodation with views of the abbey and river. *86 beds | Melrose | tel. 01896 82 25 21 | www.syha.org.uk*

▶ For a value for money breakfast look no further than *Damascus Drum Café & Bookshop* serving delicious Mediterranean cuisine, bagels, breakfasts and ☺ fair trade coffee. *Daily | 2 Silver Street, Hawick | tel. 07707 85 61 23*

▶ First-class fish and chips and award-winning, home-made ice cream at *Giacopazzi's & Oblo's Bistro* on the harbour. *Daily | at the Fish Market | Eyemouth | tel. 01890 75 25 27*

▶ The *Centre for Tibetan Buddhism* in the Esk valley offers inexpensive accommodation (and morning prayers), for longer stays there are courses in meditation, Buddhism and gardening. *Eskdalemuir | tel. 01387 37 32 32 | www.samyeling.org*

GLASGOW & SURROUNDS

MAP ON PAGES 134/135

CITY **WHERE TO START?**
From Queen Street railway station on **George Square** everything you need is within easy walking distance. The tourist office is on the square and you can reach the University of Glasgow, the School of Art and Kelvingrove Park via Buchannan and Sauchiehall Streets. The River Clyde lies south of the park. There are car parks on George Square, St Enoch Centre and at the Clyde Auditorium (known locally as the 'Armadillo') on the Clyde.

By tradition the dynamics of this city of 750,000 inhabitants (⚏ J13) is intense and loud. Glasgow blossomed 200 years ago with the deepening of the Clyde to a navigable river from its estuary to the city, a distance of 30km/18mi.

The Scottish city gained its wealth by becoming the centre of Great Britain's ship building industry. This resplendent part of its history can be gleaned from the inscriptions on the more recent burial monuments in the Necropolis cemetery; the rough part of its history is evidenced in Gorbals, the old working class neigh-

Photo: Clyde Auditorium

Welcoming, warm and down-to-earth: the shipbuilding city of Glasgow is a cultural metropolis in its own right

bourhood in the East End, which is continuously being modernized.

When the end of the era of heavy industry came about, the city met the challenge with pragmatic versatility. This was in stark contrast to Edinburgh that has always retained a very distinctive and more conservative character. Glasgow has been reinventing and redefining itself since the 1980s. Integral to this has been the communicative character of your typical Glaswegian in his shirtsleeves that visitors have come to appreciate so much, even if they struggle with the accent. Added to this, are the wit, creativity and helpfulness of its citizens.

The city has managed to become a modern metropolis without losing its robust charm. On the River Clyde an urban landscape of new buildings and bridges has sprung up.

Lions flank the town hall entrance on George Square

In the city itself *Buchanan Street* is blossoming into the UK's second-best shopping area. Neo-classical, Victorian and art nouveau façades are now free of the industrial patina of yesteryear.

Glasgow was voted European Capital of Culture in 1990 and since then students from around the world have been converging on it for its reputation as a cultural hotbed of contemporary art and music. Celtic-inspired festivals, bands like Franz Ferdinand and more recently the singer Amy MacDonald and the alternative rock band Glasvegas, have resulted in the city being bestowed the title 'Unesco City of Music' in 2008.

Glasgow was also a trendsetter in the past when the distinctive *Glasgow Style* was popularised a century ago by art nouveau designer Charles Rennie Mackintosh. Ironically Mackintosh attained greater fame abroad at the time than in his homeland. His dandyish appearance did not go down well in a city whose dynamics was based on industry. Today however his influences are all over Glasgow, be it in the two *Willow Tea Rooms (97 Buchanan Street, 217 Sauchiehall Street)* or at the *Glasgow School of Art (Renfrew Street)*.

SIGHTSEEING

CENTRE FOR CONTEMPORARY ARTS CCA (135 D2)

From poetry performances to landscaping: just about any form of contemporary art can be practised and showcased here. The focus is on the fine arts, film, music, dance and performances – but even if you're simply after a cup of coffee you will still be welcome. *350 Sauchiehall Street | Tue–Sat 11am–6pm | www.cca-glasgow.com*

GEORGE SQUARE (135 F3–4)

Glasgow's central square is surrounded by statues of poets, politicians and royalty. It is a popular spot for locals to relax at lunchtime. The square is dominated by the *City Chambers* – headquarters of the Glasgow City Council. Built of Scottish granite and

Italian marble it is well worth a visit. On a street corner south of here is *Merchant City* between Ingram Street and Tron Gate, a hip area with lovely cafés, restaurants and boutiques – meeting place of the young business and design scene.

GLASGOW SCHOOL OF ART ★ (135 D2)

It is a good idea to walk around this building, built Charles Rennie Mackintosh in 1896, before taking a look at what is behind the magnificent façade. The viewing will give you a good feel for the complete design concept of the master artist before taking in the ambiance of the renowned school. *Tours free of charge Mon–Fri at 11am and 2pm, Sat 10.30am–1pm, open house one week at the end of June | 167 Renfrew Street | www.gsa.ac.uk*

GLASGOW SCIENCE CENTRE ● (0)

State-of-the-art centre for science fans is on the newly designed river embankment – exhibitions, Imax cinema, a planetarium and the 127m/416ft high ⛷ *Glasgow Tower* all INSIDER TIP suitable for children. Opposite lies Norman Foster's *Clyde Auditorium*, known by locals as the 'Armadillo'. The best way to get there is on foot via the Clyde Walkway from Glasgow Green. *50 Pacific Quay | Tue–Fri 10am–3pm, Sat/Sun 10am–5pm | £8.25 (Glasgow Tower only £4) | www.glasgow sciencecentre.org*

HUNTERIAN MUSEUM AND ART GALLERY (134 A1)

Geological, archaeological and historical collections as well as art treasures as well and the outstanding *Mackintosh House* – a reconstruction of Charles Rennie Mackintosh's studio. *Mon–Sat 10am–5pm, Sun 2pm–5pm | admission free | University Avenue | Kelvingrove | www. hunterian.gla.ac.uk*

KELVINGROVE PARK ★ (134 A–B 1–2)

This is the most important of the city's 70 or so parks. The small Kelvin River meanders past the Glasgow Museum and Art Galleries, the Hunterian Museum and the Victorian baroque building of the University of Glasgow built in 1864 by English architect Sir Gilbert Scott. East of the park's border are houses designed by architect Charles Wilson in 1854 for well-to-do Glaswegians. You can take a 10km/6.2mi walk along the Kelvin westwards out of town. *Kelvin Way/off Kelvin Bridge*

KELVINGROVE ART GALLERY & MUSEUM ● (134 A1)

Since opening in 2006 this red sandstone building has become a tourist magnet with great artworks on display alongside interactive and informative natural science exhibits and a contemporary view of Scottish life. *Mon–Tue, Sat 10am–5pm, Fri/Sun 11am–5pm | admission free | Argyle Street Kelvingrove*

★ **Glasgow School of Art**
Tomorrow's artists study Charles Rennie Mackintosh's art nouveau style → p. 45

★ **Kelvingrove**
Glasgow's wonderful city park with a river, university and even some museums → p. 45

★ **Bute**
Once the domain of Glasgow's well-to-do – the weekend retreat with Mount Stuart House → p. 49

★ **Hill House**
Built and styled – down to the last detail – by Charles Rennie Mackintosh → p. 50

MARCO POLO HIGHLIGHTS

Victorian detail in the garden at the People's Palace

were buried with Gothic and neo-Classical monuments and sculptures, including the obelisk to the strict Anglican preacher John Knox. *Castle Street*

PEOPLE'S PALACE (0)

Opened in 1898, the city's turbulent social history is on display here in this domed building with its fabulous Victorian conservatory, the Winter Garden, in Glasgow Green public garden. Relax with a cup of tea afterwards in the park. *Mon–Thu, Sat 10am–5pm, Fri/Sun 10am–6pm| admission free | Glasgow Green East End*

RIVERSIDE MUSEUM (0)

Architectural talking point and Waterfront Renewal Project: the design by Zaha Hadid Architects cleverly incorporated the ship building industry into the building. Located on the Clyde, the new build replaces the old transport museum on the Kelvin. Steam engines, racing cars and all things transport related are on display. In front of the building is the steel-hulled Glenlee (1896) while on the opposite bank is the Govan shipyard which is building two aircraft carriers for 2014. *Mon–Thu 10am–5pm, Fri/Sun 11am–5pm | admission free | Pointhouse Place | www.glasgowmuseums.com*

THE LIGHTHOUSE ☆ (135 E4)

Designed by Charles Rennie Mackintosh for 'The Glasgow Herald' in 1895, it was launched in 1999 as the *Scotland Centre for Architecture, Design and the City*. The tower has excellent views of the city and it also houses a design shop, exhibits, a Mackintosh information centre and a café. *Mitchell Lane/Buchanan Street | Mon –Sat 10.30am–5pm, Tue until 11pm, Sun noon–5pm | £3 | www.thelighthouse.co.uk*

NECROPOLIS ● ☆ (0)

There are uninterrupted views of the city from this expansive hill-top cemetery near Glasgow's cathedral. Walk around the cemetery and you'll get a perspective on how the citizens of the city's Victorian era

CORINTHIAN (135 F4)

Centrally located in Merchant City, serving inspired fusion cuisine in an atmosphere of elegance and urban ease. Go there for lunch at least. *Daily | 191 Ingram Street | tel. 0141 5 52 11 01 | Moderate–Expensive*

CRABBSHAKK (134 A2)

Cosy, cabin charm on three floors. Seafood galore served: treat yourself to oysters and champagne and fish and chips served in style. Delicious! *Closed Mon | 1114 Argyle Street | tel. 0141 3 34 61 27 | Moderate*

GANDOLFI FISH (135 F4)

This elegant restaurant serves seafood from the Hebrides, which is also where head chef Jamie Donald hails from. He was named the Scottish 'Chef of the Year' in 2009. A few doors further on is Café Gandolfi *(64 | Albion Street | tel. 0141 552 68 13 | Budget)* a culinary institution – it has been going strong for 30 years – with a charming bar. INSIDER**TIP** See website for cooking demonstations (click on 'about') . *Daily | 84–86 Albion Street | tel. 0141 552 94 75 | www.cafegandolfi. com | Moderate*

MOTHER INDIA (134 A2)

Possibly the best Indian restaurant north of London. Let the fragrant smells seduce you, enjoy an Indian beer or take along your own bottle of wine for a small corkage fee. *Daily | Westminster Terrace | tel. 0141 221 16 63 | Budget*

INSIDER**TIP** **THE UBIQUITOUS CHIP** (0)

This restaurant is as Scottish as it gets and they also note where their fish, beef or dessert ingredients have been sourced from. A less pricy option is the bistro *(Budget)* upstairs. *Daily | 12 Ashton Lane | tel. 0141 3 34 50 07 | www.ubiquitouschip. co.uk | Moderate–Expensive*

SHOPPING

Glasgow has earned its reputation as a shopping magnet and its *Buchanan Street* is on a par with London's Regent Street. Leading off from it is *Princes Square*, an elegant shopping mall with top designers such as Vivienne Westwood. Creative force *Camille Lorigo* from New York has opened a fashion showroom on the sixth floor of Argyll Arcade off Buchanan Street. The monthly *Glasgow Craft Mafia* market *(Café Mono, King's Court | dates at: www. glasgowcraftmafia.com)* sells unique and wonderful arts and crafts. Trendy designer stores have now moved into the sandstone buildings of *Merchant City* between Trongate and Ingram Street while the boutiques of the West End are elegant and chic but not as hip. Off-beat conceptual design art is the domain of the *Transmission Gallery (28 King Street)* while *Goodd (11 James Morrison Street)* sells witty household items. *Trongate 103 Arts Centre* showcases various creative disciplines across six floors *(Trongate 103)*.

ENTERTAINMENT

THE ARCHES (135 E4)

There is always something on offer in The Arches beneath Glasgow Central railway station. A bar, arts venue and theatre and night club will leave you spoilt for choice with their repertoire of gigs and events. Top-notch sound. *253 Argyle Street | tel. 0141 221 40 01 | www.thearches.co.uk*

LOW BUDGET

▶ Why not first decide how much you are willing to spend on dinner and then place a bid under *www. priceyourmeal.com* where you can secure a seat in a restaurant via auction (also in Edinburgh).

▶ The *Discovery Subway Ticket* only costs £3.50 and is valid the whole day from 9.30am (Sun all day) for the entire underground network.

▶ Low budget stay? For affordable rates of accommodation check out the Glasgow City Marketing Bureau website: *www.seaglasgow. com/hotels*

INSIDER TIP ▶ BEN NEVIS (134 A2)

Celtic-style local pub in the West End. The owner is from the Highlands and has decorated his whisky emporium (180 types!) in the traditional style. For a Scotch at its Scottish best! *Daily | 1197 Argyle Street*

KING TUT'S WAH WAH HUT (135 D3)

Sweaty walls and on trend music, this is the UK's top address for the club scene. To make it as a band you have to have a gig here. *Daily | 272 St Vincent Street | tel. 0141 2 21 52 79 | www.kingtuts.co.uk*

NICE 'N' SLEAZY (135 D2)

Their reputation for big burgers *(Budget)* and cool jukebox music means you can't go wrong here – live gigs and hip dance floor. *Daily | 421 Sauchiehall Street | tel. 0141 3 33 96 37 | www.nicensleazy.com*

ORAN MOR (0)

This converted parish church is now a multi-purpose venue and behind its façades are two restaurants, two bars, a private dining room and a nightclub. The auditorium is magnificent and its beautiful celestial ceiling mural will make you feel a little closer to the heavens. *Daily | Byres Road/Great Western Road | tel. 0141 3 57 62 26 | www.oran-mor.co.uk*

INSIDER TIP ▶ SCOTIA BAR & CLUTHA VAULTS (135 F5)

Two small pubs opposite one another offering excellent rock, blues and poetry slams. Beer and stories flow freely and it's easy to strike up a conversation. *Daily | 167 Stockwell St. | tel. 0141 5 52 86 81 (Scotia Bar) and 0141 5 52 75 20 (Clutha Vaults)*

WHERE TO STAY

INSIDER TIP ▶ BABBITY BOWSTER (0)

Lovely rooms above one the nicest pubs in town. Before you go to sleep you can head downstairs for a whisky nightcap a chat. Top location in Merchant City so booking is essential! *6 rooms | 16–18 Blackfriars Street | tel. 0141 5 52 50 55 | Budget–Moderate*

BELGRAVE HOTEL (0)

Clean and reasonable, in a typical Georgian townhouse in the West End. *12 rooms | 2 Belgrave Terrace, Great Western Road | tel. 0141 3 37 18 50 | www.belgraveguesthouse.co.uk | Budget*

CITY INN (135 F4)

Big, modern hotel in a good location on the Clyde with a post-industrial harbour vibe. Pleasing design, small rooms but they come with a balcony. Café restaurant on the terrace *(Budget)*. *164 rooms | Finnieston Quay | tel. 0141 24 01 00 02 | www.cityinn.com/glasgow | Moderate*

MANOR PARK HOTEL (0)

Small townhouse hotel in the West End with a park across from it. Hearty breakfasts, excellent Scottish hospitality and good parking. *10 rooms | 28 Belshagray Drive | tel. 0141 3 39 21 43 | www.manorparkhotel.com | Budget*

THE MERCHANT LODGE (135 F4)

Simple but neat rooms in what used to be the home of a tobacco merchant, centrally located in Merchant City. No porter, so be prepared to carry your suitcase up the stairs. *40 rooms | 52 Virginia Street | tel. 0141 5 52 24 24 | Budget*

MILLENNIUM HOTEL (135 F3)

Prominent location on George Square next to Queen Street Station. 4 stars, spacious rooms with all conveniences and breakfast served in the conservatory overlooking the square. *110 rooms | 40 George Square | tel. 0141 3 32 67 11 | www.millenniumhotels.com | Moderate*

INFORMATION

TOURIST INFORMATION CENTRE
(135 F4)
11 George Square | tel. 0141 2 04 44 80 | www.seeglasgow.com

WHERE TO GO

ARRAN
(120–121 C–D 2–3) *(⬦ G13–14)*

This remote island is a miniature version of Scotland: it has mountains (the 874m/2867ft *Goat Fell*); standing stones (on the Machrie Moor); a castle (in *Brodick* town) and a small, modern whisky distillery – its ten year old malt is one of the best. The best way to explore Arran is by hiring a bicycle. Also on offer: sea kayaking, gorge scrambling, rock climbing and more *(www.arranadventure.com)*. Auchrannie Resort

(85 rooms | tel. 01770 30 22 34 | www.auchrannie.co.uk | Moderate) or Kilmichael House *(7 rooms | tel. 01770 30 22 19 | www.kilmichael.com | Expensive)* are two good accommodation options. Arran is also the perfect INSIDER TIP springboard to the distant Kintyre peninsula. *The car ferry from Ardrossan (25km/15.5mi west of Glasgow) to Brodick runs 6 times daily from Mon–Sat, the Lochranza–Claonaig (Kintyre) car ferry 9 times daily | tel. 01770 30 21 66*

BUTE ★ (121 D1–2) *(⬦ G13)*

This small island is in close proximity to Glasgow, it is a half hour train journey from Central Station to Wemyss Bay, followed by another half hour by ferry. After the introduction of the steam ship in the 19th century, *Rothesay* port became a popular weekend destination for well

Off the beaten track: the Isle of Arran is a miniature version of Scotland

heeled Glaswegians. However, in 1910 when holidays for the working classes were introduced, Rothesay lost its exclusivity. Make the *Victorian Toilets* at the harbour your first port of call – still in use today they are bound to make you smile. Next take a stroll through the town of Rothesay then head to the east coast's ● *Mount Stuart House (tours Easter and May–Aug Mon–Fri 11am–4pm, Sat/Sun 11am–2pm | £8 | www.mountstuart.com)*. The interior of the Gothic Revival red sandstone castle is the most esoteric and romantic in Scotland. Its last owner had a passion for Catholicism, astronomy and astrology – reflected in the magnificent marble chapel, the impressive entrance hall and the mythological detail in the rooms.

HILL HOUSE ⭐ (121 E1) (*⌖ H12*)

An hour's drive from Glasgow, this house in Helensburgh was designed in detail by Charles Rennie Mackintosh and his wife. It was built in 1904 for publisher Walter Blackie and shows the Scottish art nouveau style with typical colours, wall hangings and décor. Also with tea garden, a library and a shop selling INSIDER TIP ▸ fun souvenirs by young Scottish designers: the ingredients for a perfect day out. *Mon–Sat 10.30am–5.30pm, Sun noon–5pm | Helensburgh | 45km/28mi north-west of Glasgow*

HOLY ISLAND ● (121 D3) (*⌖ G14*)

Some 1400 years ago a monk by the name of St Molaise lived as a hermit on this island east of Arran. Legend has it that he accepted 30 deadly diseases to avoid purgatory. Monks are once again living on Holy Island after Buddhists arrived in the 1960s. Their monastery, Samyé Ling, became famous despite its isolation: John Lennon and Leonard Cohen came here on a visit as did David Bowie who apparently even considered becoming a monk. The monastery is now a spiritual centre. Guests, including day visitors, are most welcome and can participate in meditation and prayers, even spend the night. There is a beautiful mandala garden and everywhere you get a strong sense that there is hope for world peace. *65 beds | tel. 01770 70 04 63 | www.holyisland.org | Budget*

SCOTTISH BASICS

aber:	river mouth	*kyle:*	strait
aig:	bay	*loch:*	lake
bal:	village	*rannoch:*	fern
beag:	small	*sassenach:*	an English person
ben:	mountain, mountain range	*sgian dubh:*	small dagger tucked into knee-high hose
bie, by:	farmstead	*strath:*	wide valley
bonny:	pretty	*tarbert:*	headland
cairn:	mound of stones	*tattie:*	potato
craig:	rocks	*trews:*	tartan trousers
firth:	inlet	*vik, wick:*	bay
glen:	narrow valley	*voe:*	a small bay or creek

INSIDER TIP ▶ **KINTYRE**
(120 B–C 3–4) (*🛱 F14*)

The most south-westerly peninsula well off the beaten track and seldom included in tours, and this is despite the famous

The industrial capitalists deployed children to operate the heavy machinery and they constituted 70 per cent of the labour force. It had become obvious to Owen that well treated, educated and healthy

Hill House in Helensburgh: the perfect example of Scottish art nouveau

Paul McCartney song, 'Mull of Kintyre'. However, whisky connoisseurs come here to vistit the three distilleries *Springbank, Glen Scotia* and *Glengyle.* Golfers also come here to try their hand at the *Machrihanish Golf Club* and its famously difficult first hole (*www.machgolf.com*) while nature lovers and hikers love the 8km/5mi *Machrihanish* beach from where you can see Ireland. *Approx. 200 km/124mi west of Glasgow*

NEW LANARK (122 B3) (*🛱 K13*)

Robert Owen (1771–1858) was an industrialist and social reformer. The conditions in the cotton mills – while state-of-the art in his time – were crying out for reform.

workers would mean higher profits. So, he improved their living conditions and increased the breaks of his 2500-strong operational workforce and also established a school and introduced health care and cultural activities in the workplace. His pioneering social model and the details and care with which he ran his organisation are documented in the New Lanark World Heritage site and museum. A good over night option is at the *Mill Hotel* built in an old spinning mill (*38 rooms | tel. 01555 66 72 00 | Moderate*) directly on the River Clyde. *Daily 11am–5pm| www.newlanark.org | 50km/31mi south-east of Glasgow*

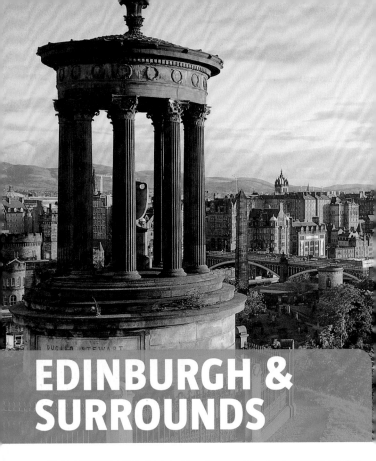

EDINBURGH & SURROUNDS

CITY **WHERE TO START?**
Waverley Station: the city's main station is within easy walking distance of the Old Town with the Royal Mile, New Town and Princes Street. The airport bus also stops at this station. For parking head straight to Waverley, the Castle or St James shopping centre in New Town.

MAP INSIDE BACK COVER
When people think of Edinburgh (127 D6) (*M K–L12*) they think of haggis, bagpipes and Dr Jekyll and Mr Hyde but the new millennium heralded in a revival and the city seems to have awoken from its deep beauty sleep.

Even though Edinburgh (pop. 450,000) is smaller than Glasgow, Scotland's capital sets the country's pace in every respect – not only when it comes to politics. Aside from its famous festivals, Edinburgh boasts a revamped port, boutique hotels, stylish clubs, exclusive shopping emporiums, Michelin star cuisine and the remarkable new houses of parliament right in the middle of its historical centre – now a World Heritage Site. Edinburgh's skyline is highlighted by the dramatic *Edinburgh Castle* perched up high, overlooking the

Photo: The Dugald Stewart Monument on Calton Hill

Majestic with a touch of nostalgia: Edinburgh has always been and still is the diva of Scottish towns

city. Spread out directly below it is *Old Town*, the historic centre of Edinburgh with its winding alleys, pubs and tall, narrow 16th and 17th century buildings once frequented by the likes Sir Walter Scott, philosopher David Hume and painter Henry Raeburn. The *New Town* area dates from the 18th century and the Georgian era and is characterised by wide, generous streets and squares – *Charlotte Square* is one the city's most elegant squares. Edinburgh is still inspiring, especially because of its growing literary scene. Author Ian Rankin used the city as the inspiration for his books, as did J. K. Rowling the author of the best-selling 'Harry Potter' novels. She wrote the first volume of the series in a café in Edinburgh, not unusual because writing has always been a tradition in this city. Robert Burns, Sir Walter Scott and

Robert Louis Stevenson all lived in the city and all left their mark not only in their books but also in the exhibits at the *Writers' Museum.* The narrative tradition and love for it, is continued today at the INSIDER**TIP** *The Scottish Storytelling Centre* in *John Knox House* with its fascinating exhibits and readings *(Mon–Sat 10am–*

Scottish coats of arms displayed in the castle

6pm | 43 High Street | www.scottishstory tellingcentre.co.uk). Every year in August Edinburgh reminds its citizens and visitors alike of its special relationship with literature when it celebrates the *Book Festival (www.edbookfest.co.uk)* where hundreds of well-known authors take centre stage. But it is not only when it comes to literature that Edinburgh has a say: for centuries this Scottish city had been rendered insignificant when it came to politics but all that changed in 1999 when partial autonomy allowed for the election of the new Scottish Parliament, much to the joy of its citizens. In 2004 the new 430 million pound parliament building, designed by Catalan architect Enric Miralles, was completed.

CALTON HILL ● ☼ (U E3) (*∭ e3*)

The two best views of the city are east of Edinburgh city centre. The green *Calton Hill* (100m/328ft) is littered with grandiose monuments from the first half of the 19th century such as the *Old Royal High School,* the *Dugald Stewart Monument* and the unfinished war memorial, the *National Monument.*

Some 2km/1.2mi beyond Holyrood and the Scottish Parliament is the 251m/823ft high *Arthur's Seat.* A hill that is actually the basalt core of a 350 million year old volcano. The steep climb gives you stunning views of the parliament buildings and west over the cityscape.

CHARLOTTE SQUARE (U B4) (*∭ b4*)

Georgian style par excellence: architect Robert Adams designed this stylish square in New Town – a Unesco World Heritage Site. The *Georgian House* museum (no. 7) displays the lifestyle of the upper-classes in the 18th and 19th century *(March/Nov daily 11am–3pm, April–Jun, Sept/Oct 10am–5pm, July–Aug 10am–7pm | £5.50).* Today the Scottish head of government resides next door (No. 6) so it is a common sight to see politicians and lobbyists having lunch at the café below the *Trust for Scotland* gallery (no. 28) with its beautiful Georgian parquet floor. *Café Mon–Sat 9.30am–5.30pm*

EDINBURGH CASTLE ★ (U C4) (*∭ c4*)

A trip to Edinburgh would not be complete without a visit to the castle. Its chapel dates as far back as the 12th century, its main building is from the 18th and 19th century and its walls contain the *Scottish National War Museum,* the Scottish crown jewels and the *Stone of Destiny* – used in the coronation ceremonies of the Scottish monarchs.

In August, the castle becomes the focal point of the *Military Tattoo,* opening with a military parade at the castle and culminating in a massive street festival *(www.edintattoo.co.uk). April–Oct daily 9.30am–6pm, Nov–March 9.30am–5pm | £11 | Castlehill | www.edinburghcastle.co.uk*

GREYFRIARS KIRKYARD ●
(U D5) (*m d5*)

Just inside the gate of this cemetery is the grave of a Skye terrier called Bobby. Legend has it that after his master was buried here in 1858 the loyal dog spent the next 14 years guarding his grave until he died in 1872. Take a guided tour to hear stories like the 'Greyfriars Bobby' as well as those of William Burke and William Hare. They were two men who dug up freshly buried bodies to sell to Edinburgh's Institute of Anatomical Research. When demand exceeded supply they gave in to temptation and the two men became serial killers. They murdered at least 16 people before they were caught. *Daily | Candlemaker Row/Chambers Street*

LEITH RIVER (0)

A walk west of New Town along the River Leith through the Edinburgh suburbs of Stockbridge and Dean Village takes you into an area of rural charm. The river flows through a green canyon – a INSIDER TIP superb jogging route – and a short climb up gets you to an unexpected art haven: the *Dean Gallery* and *National Gallery of Modern Art* exhibit works from the 19th century to present day, the former is also home to the works of Eduardo Paolozzi (1924–2005), Edinburgh's top artist. Next to the galleries is INSIDER TIP *Dean Cemetery* in full grandeur. *Galleries daily noon–5pm | admission free | 75 Belford Road | www.nationalgalleries.org*

NATIONAL GALLERIES OF SCOTLAND
(U C4) (*m c4*)

Whatever art period inspires you, Edinburgh is bound to have the appropriate gallery. The *National Gallery of Scotland,* whose Doric columns are reminiscent of ancient temples, is ideally located between Old Town and New Town. Since 1859 this neo-Classical bastion of art has reflected the city's claim for taking science and culture to centre stage. Inside you will find the history of painting on its crowded walls – from Holbein to Goya and Van Gogh to Cézanne. Connected to the gallery is the more modern *Royal Scottish*

Impressive display of art treasures at the National Gallery

Academy Building showing special exhibitions. January is the only month that the curators put the highly sensitive INSIDER TIP William Turner watercolours on display – the rest of the year they are locked away to save them from exposure to daylight. *Fri–Wed 10am–5pm, Thu 10am–7pm | admission free | The Mound | www.nationalgalleries.org*

NATIONAL MUSEUM OF SCOTLAND
(U D5) (𝄞 d5)

The convex new sandstone façade opposite the somewhat mysterious *Greyfriars Kirkyard* is a strong statement of modern-day Scotland. Inside, Scotland is presented in a contemporary way that goes beyond the clichés – everything from witches and relics to information about Dolly the cloned sheep. The ☕ *Tower Restaurant (daily noon–11pm | tel. 0131 2 25 30 03 | www.towerrestaurant.com | Moderate)* has spectacular views of the city. *Daily 10am–5pm | admission free | Chambers Street | www.nms.ac.uk*

PALACE OF HOLYROODHOUSE
(U F4) (𝄞 f4)

'Queenie's timeshare' is what the locals jokingly call it. The queen does indeed only spend one week a year in her official residence in Scotland. An abbey in the 12th century it became the royal seat 400 years later. Robert Louis Stevenson wrote, 'Holyrood is a house of many memories. Wars have been plotted, dancing has lasted deep into the night, murder has been done in its chambers.' *April–Oct daily 9.30am–6pm, Nov–March 9.30am–4.30pm | £10 | Canongate | www.royal collection.org.uk*

ROYAL BOTANIC GARDEN ★ ●
(U B1) (𝄞 b1)

The Victorian Palm House – the largest in the United Kingdom – is its focal point. It houses 2400 species of 5400 plants and has ongoing exhibitions like that of Scottish artist, philosopher and landscaper Ian Hamilton Finlay. *Nov–Feb daily 10am–4pm, March until 6pm, April–Sept until*

7pm, Oct until 6pm | admission free | 20 A Inverleith Row | www.rbge.org.uk

THE ROYAL MILE ★ ●
(U C3–F4) (*ꟷ c3–f4*)

This is probably the world's most dramatic historic street: in the 18th century some 60,000 people lived along the Mile in buildings that were up to 15 floors high. Lawyers, prostitutes, wealthy citizens and poor men alike made their way through its filth and sewage, while the likes of philosopher David Hume and poet Robert Ferguson – whose statues adorn the route – would ponder the dire state of affairs. History is in evidence everywhere here including the home of Calvinist reformer John Knox who clashed with fun-loving Catholic Mary Queen of Scots. Look out for the pub that bears Deacon Brodie's name, an Edinburgh citizen whose double life inspired author Robert Louis Stevenson's novel 'Dr. Jekyll and Mr. Hyde'.

Today thousands upon thousands of visitors make their way across its old cobbled pavements leading downhill from Castle Hill to the Palace of Holyrood via High Street on to Canongate. Along the way are all things Scottish: kilts, whisky, bagpipes, oatmeal biscuits and – on a guided tour – scary anecdotes → *p. 104*.

ROYAL YACHT BRITANNIA (U F1) (*ꟷ f1*)

Even Margaret Rutherford the 'Miss Marple' actress has been on board. After 44 years in service the Britannia is now anchored on the River Leith. An audio tour accompanies a visit through its five decks. *April–Sept daily 9.30am–4.30pm, Oct–March 10am–3.30pm | £9.50 | Ocean Terminal Leith | www.royalyachtbritannia.co.uk*

THE SCOTTISH PARLIAMENT ★
(U F4) (*ꟷ f4*)

After its opening in 2004 the highly controversial parliamentary building now has record numbers of visitors. Its poetic modern architecture integrates elements of the Scottish countryside with Edinburgh's distinctive old alleyways in an ingenious and unobtrusive way. Highly recommended: INSIDER TIP book a tour on a day when parliament is not in session. Parliament with its 129 officials sits in the plenary session building on Wed and Thu. *Mon/Fri 10am–5.30pm (Oct–March until 4pm), Tue–Thu 9am–6.30pm, Sat 11am–5.30pm | admission free, tours £5 | Holyrood Road | tel. 0131 3 48 52 00 | www.scottish.parliament.uk*

ST GILES CATHEDRAL (U D4) (*ꟷ d4*)

The compact Mother Church of Scottish Presbyterianism is prominent on the Royal Mile. The columns in its sanctuary date back to 1120 and are its oldest architectural relics. When the English destroyed the church, it was rebuilt with strict dimensions in the Gothic architectural style, providing the perfect stage for the inflammatory sermons of reformer John Knox (1514–72) who preached at the church for twelve years. In 2010 St Giles was refurbished and today's visitors can once again admire the shining marble altar and the inner portal with its iridescent blue glass. The chapel of the Scottish Order of the Thistle, added in 1911, is a real treasure chest of exquisite woodwork and carved masonry. The Queen, as Sovereign, and her offspring Prince Charles and Princess Anne are members and bring up the number of 16 knights to the total of 19. Each Thistle knight has their own seat decorated with their coats of arms. Commoners have to have one designed before they can be admitted to the Order and are then seated in the stalls. While some of the knights' statues look quite bizarre, the cathedral's most curious treasure has to be that of two angels playing the bagpipes. *April–Sept daily 9am–*

7pm, Oct–March 9am–5pm | admission free | Royal Mile/Lawnmarket

WRITERS' MUSEUM
(U D4) (𝄞 d4)

Manuscripts, quill pens, Robert Burns' desk – a museum that combines the weird and wonderful with the writings of the big three literary icons: Robert Burns, Sir Walter Scott and Robert Louis Stevenson. *Mon–Sat 10am–5pm, Aug also Sun noon–5pm | admission free | Lady Stair's Close, Lawnmarket | Royal Mile*

FOOD & DRINK

THE DOGS (U C3) (𝄞 c3)

Wacky New Town vibe with kitsch and arty dog theme décor. Cheap, simple, and good food, cosy and often full. *Daily | 110 Hanover Street | tel. 0131 2 20 12 08 | www.thedogsonline.co.uk | Budget*

INSIDER TIP ▶ THE GRAIN STORE
(U D5) (𝄞 d5)

The atmosphere inside its old stone walls and attentive service makes it deserving

of five stars. Great restaurant with moderate prices – as has been the case for 20 years now. The kitchen even manages to refine black pudding. *Daily | 30 Victoria Street | tel. 0131 2 25 76 35 | Budget–Moderate*

OLIVE BRANCH (U D2) (𝄞 d2)

Café-style restaurant in Broughton, the neighbourhood with a strong gay scene. Colourful bunch of people, generous portions of mostly fried or deep-fried foods. Try the INSIDER TIP ▶ Sunday brunch. *Daily | 91 Broughton Street | tel. 0131 5 57 85 89 | www.theolivebranch.co.uk | Budget*

RESTAURANT MARTIN WISHART ★
(0)

Head chef Martin Wishart has been holding on to his Michelin star since 2001. His cuisine is rated as the best in Edinburgh, if not in Scotland. Pleasant, simple interior! *Closed Sun/Mon | 54 The Shore Leith | tel. 0131 5 53 35 57 | www.martin-wishart.co.uk | Expensive*

THE RUTLAND HOTEL RESTAURANT
(U B4) (𝄞 b4)

Located at the foot of the castle in the West End is the city's new favourite restaurant. Its food and wine are top class and there are some great window seats or secluded nooks for a INSIDER TIP ▶ romantic dinner. *Daily | 1 Rutland Street | tel. 0131 22 93 40 21 | www.therutlandhotel.com | Moderate*

SHOPPING

New Town's most fashionable street would have to be *George Street* (U B4–C3) (𝄞 b4–c3). Here row upon row of dignified building façades invite window shoppers and shoppers alike. At its most eastern end is the newly refurbished St Andrew's Square (U D3) (𝄞 d3). *Harvey*

LOW BUDGET

▶ The *Halfway House* pub is tucked away between the Royal Mile and the railway station up a steep, narrow alley. Offering delicious traditional, home-made food, good beer and warm atmosphere. *Daily | 24 Fleshmarket Close*

▶ Take a closer look: it's worth checking out the back of your bus ticket for discounts on entrance fees to exhibitions or for fast food chains.

Shoppers' haven Edinburgh: a unique handbag as a special souvenir

Nichols opened its exclusive department store here and has drawn other luxury brands into the area – especially to Multrees Walk.

If delightfully eccentric clothing and recycled fashions are your thing, then *Joey D (www.joey-d.co.uk)* in Broughton Street (U D2) *(𝄞 d2)* is just the place for you. Why not take home one of their outlandish and unconventional handbags.

Princes Street (U B–D4) *(𝄞 b–d4)* divides your shopping excursion into a New Town and Old Town experience. You'll find shop upon shop in the northern stretch of this boulevard with the southern stretch opening up to the fantastic skyline of Old Town and to the *Princes Street Gardens* – the best spot to relax after you've done all your shopping. Princes Street is also where you'll find the labyrinth of shops that make up the traditional department store *Jenners. Cockburn Street* (U D4) is for music fans with its well-stocked shops. Now that you've reached Old Town, look out for whisky and tartan in the Royal Mile shops. Even more exciting are the concentration of small INSIDER TIP independent shops surrounding Grassmarket and Victoria Street – terrific fashion, second-hand kilts, imaginative hats, modern knitwear and more (U C–D5) *(𝄞 c–d5)*.

ENTERTAINMENT

CAFÉ ROYAL BAR (U D3) *(𝄞 d3)*
Great pub with opulent Victorian interior and tile art dating back to 1886. Adjoining it is a good seafood restaurant. *17 West Register Street | www.caferoyal.org.uk*

EGO (U D3) *(𝄞 d3)*
Locals currently rate Ego as Edinburgh's best dance club. It has a magnificent ballroom with high ceiling, but also smaller halls for house and techno fans. Good gay scene. *14 Picardy Place | www.clubego.co.uk*

GEORGE STREET
(U B–C 3–4) *(𝄞 b–c 3–4)*
This exclusive Edinburgh area also has the coolest cocktail bars such as *Opal Lounge (51 George Street)*, *Tigerlily (125 George*

Street) and *Rick's (55a Frederick Street)*. If you prefer less hustle and bustle try the *Outhouse (12 Broughton Street Lane)* in the relaxed Broughton neighbourhood.

LEITH (0)

The old harbour area of Leith has evolved into a popular part of the city for eating and drinking with three of its fashionable restaurants having Michelin stars. There are also the tried and trusted gastropubs offering good culinary fare such as *King's Wark (The Shore)* and the friendly bistro-bar *The Shore (3 The Shore)* with its harbour view.

SANDY BELL'S ● (U D5) (*ⵎ d5*)

Some of the city's best folk musicians frequent this unpretentious music pub for a beer, enriching the evening jam sessions with the sounds of their fiddles and accordions. *Daily | 25 Forrest Road*

THE BALMORAL (U C4) (*ⵎ c4*)

A home away from home to the stars, this palatial building with its clock tower stands out on the eastern end of Princes Street. Its luxury extends to its spa and Michelin star restaurant, *Number One*. It all comes at a price of course: double rooms from £150. *188 rooms | 1 Princes Street | tel. 0131 5 56 24 14 | www.thebalmoral hotel.com | Expensive*

BALMORE HOUSE (U B6) (*ⵎ b6*)

Friendly guest house with Victorian décor. Its sister establishment, Bowmore with its wooden floors, has a Scandinavian feel. Hearty breakfasts. *7 rooms | 34 Gilmore Place | tel. 0131 2 2113 31 | Budget*

CHANNINGS (U A2) (*ⵎ a2*)

Elegant and steeped in history: five Georgian townhouses have been com-

bined into a hotel. Some once belonged to polar explorer Sir Ernest Shackleton – expedition photos are on display in some of the rooms. Excellent restaurant. *41 rooms | 12–16 South Learmonth Gardens | tel. 0131 2 74 74 01 | www.channings.co.uk | Expensive*

HOTEL DU VIN (U D5) (*ⵎ d5*)

A boutique hotel in a historical Old Town building with a superb bistro restaurant and lovely rooms. Plus: cigar lounge, wine bar and **INSIDER TIP** whisky tasting room (reservations essential). The building was once an asylum and the poet Robert Fergusson died here at the age of 24. *47 rooms | 11 Bristo Place | tel. 0131 2 47 49 00 | www.hotelduvin.com | Moderate–Expensive*

HUDSON HOTEL (U B4) (*ⵎ b4*)

Hip, urban hotel with modern rooms in the West End. Great location at the junction between Old Town, New Town and Dean Village with a bus connection to the airport. *30 rooms | 9–11 Hope Street | tel. 0131 2 47 70 00 | www.thehudsonhotel. co.uk | Moderate*

MALMAISON (0)

One of the city's older designer hotels, charming atmosphere. *100 rooms | 12/1 Tower Place, Leith | tel. 0131 4 69 50 00 | www.malmaison-edinburgh.com | Moderate–Expensive*

SHERATON GRAND HOTEL ● (U B5) (*ⵎ b5*)

After undergoing a complete renovation its grandeur shines once again. Its most expensive rooms overlook the castle and it boasts the best spa in the capital (also for non-residents). In addition to the usual fitness classes and gym facilities, treatments using hot stones and ayurvedic techniques are also offered, as are

Mighty Linlithgow Palace: ancestral seat of the Stuarts

facials, manicures and massages. The superb swimming pool stretches right to the edge of the roof. *269 rooms | 1 Festival Square | tel. 0131 2 21 77 77 | www.starwood hotels.com/sheraton | www.one-spa.net | Expensive*

EDINBURGH & SCOTLAND INFORMATION CENTRE (U C4) (*🕮 c4*)
3 Princes Street | tel. 0845 2 25 51 21 (*) | www.edinburgh.org

WHERE TO GO

THE FORTH RAIL BRIDGE
(126 C6) (*🕮 K12*)
A true landmark completed in 1890 it spans the Firth of Forth with its grandiose timber framework trusses and 6.5 million steel rivets *(www.forthbridges.org.uk)*. Take the train from Waverley to Dalmeny. *20km/12mi west of Edinburgh*

LINLITHGOW PALACE (122 C1) (*🕮 K12*)
Documented for the first time in 1301, Linlithgow Palace was the birthplace of Mary, Queen of Scots. The picturesque castle ruins are in a park. *End March–Sept daily 9.30am–5.30pm, Oct–beginning March until 4.30pm | entrance fee £5.50 | www.historic-scotland.gov.uk | M9 | 25km/ 15.5mi west of Edinburgh*

ROSSLYN CHAPEL ★ (123 D2) (*🕮 L13*)
There are many legends surrounding this 15th century chapel. It is also the setting for the denouement of Dan Brown's bestseller 'The Da Vinci Code'. Centre of attention is the *Apprentice Pillar* and some mysterious stone carvings – possibly encoded musical scores. In 2007 the musician Stuart Mitchell translated these into 'The Rosslyn Motet'. *April–Sept Mon–Sat 9.30am–6pm, Sun noon–4.45pm, Oct–March 9.30am–5pm, Sun noon–4.45pm | £8 | 12km/7.4mi south of Edinburgh | www. rosslynchapel.org.uk*

THE HIGHLANDS

The Scottish Highlands is the region where the Lowlands end and where golf is *the* sport, where national hero Rob Roy is honoured to this day and where pub patrons lower their voices if there is talk of the place where the Scottish kings were once crowned: **Scone Palace near Perth.** Rising up directly behind the Highlands are the *Grampian Mountains*. A region that has become instrumental in shaping the popular image of Scotland: desolate and dramatic plateaus, windswept heather and scattered sheep and majestic historic sites like *Glencoe*, (the 'Valley of Tears') and legendary *Loch Ness*. While *Royal Deeside* in the east lures visitors with its castles and distilleries, the northern Highlands are far more sparsely populated where villages consist of only a handful of houses and the coastline is wild and rugged.

ABERDEEN

(127 F1) *(Ⓜ N8)* Also poetically designated as the 'Silver City by the Sea' – Aberdeen is on a bay between the mouths of the Don and Dee rivers – and is Scotland's third-largest city with a population of 185,000.
Ranked behind Glasgow and Edinburgh it still leads a Cinderella existence even

Photo: View over Loch Affric to Glen Affric

**Myths and clichés:
this is where men wear kilts and
the Royal Family like to holiday**

though its town privileges date way back to 1179. Today offshore oil has turned Aberdeen into Europe's oil capital.

The city also attracted worldwide interest because of its granite. The local deposits of this silver-grey stone are one the world's best granite types. Aside from being used in housing construction in Aberdeen, it has been used worldwide from the streets of London to the piers of Rio de Janeiro.

In the 19th century its coastal location made shipbuilding an important economic factor in Aberdeen.

FOOTDEE

A fishing village that was built 200 years ago by the architect of Balmoral Castle, Footdee is on the coast where the River

ABERDEEN

Dee flows into the sea. At the time the residents of Footdee (pronounced: Fittie) were fishermen but today it is home to a colourful mix of people and professions. This village-like outpost is about a half hour walk from Aberdeen city centre. The path leads along the busy Victoria Dock

FOOD & DRINK

BLUE MOON
A modern Indian restaurant serving delicious, freshly made curries. *Daily | 11 Holburn Street | tel. 01224 58 99 77 | www. bluemoon-aberdeen.com | Budget*

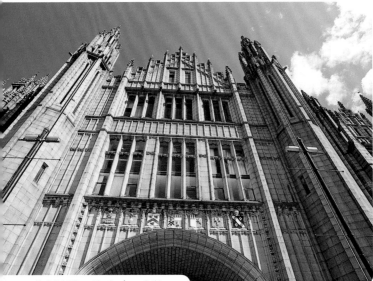

Marischal College: Aberdeen's neo-Gothic gem

harbour with its huge warehouses, containers and silos. *Quay East*

MARISCHAL COLLEGE
The world's largest granite building was built here in 1837 for the university and you'd be forgiven for mistaking it for a cathedral. It now houses the municipal offices. *Broad Street*

MARITIME MUSEUM
Exhibits about shipping, navigation and life on the oil platforms. *Mon–Sat 10am– 5pm, Sun 11.30am–5pm | admission free | 19 Justice Mill Lane*

SILVER DARLING
One of Scotland's best seafood restaurants is right here in Footdee, perched over the Dee estuary in what was once the outlook of the Aberdeen harbour pilot. *Closed Sun | tel. 01224 57 62 29 | www. silverdarling.co.uk | Expensive*

ENTERTAINMENT

THE LEMON TREE
Stage for live excellent alternative performances. Opens just before the evening show. Try the INSIDER**TIP** lunchtime acts from Fri–Sun. *Daily | 5 West North Street |*

tel. 01224 6 41 | www.boxofficeaberdeen. com

WHERE TO STAY

THE GLOBE INN
Lively good and inexpensive hotel with clean rooms, above a pub serving excellent cuisine that attracts a nice crowd. *7 rooms | 13–15 North Silver Street | tel. 01224 62 42 58 | Budget*

HILTON GARDEN INN
Modern, centrally located luxury hotel with some nice touches such as large rain showers, adjustable beds, a gym and a sumptuous breakfast. *110 rooms | 31 St Andrew Street | 01224 45 14 44 | http:// hiltongardeninn.hilton.co.uk | Moderate*

INFORMATION

ABERDEEN VISITOR INFORMATION
23 Union Street | tel. 01224 28 88 28 | www.aberdeenhq.com

WHERE TO GO

BALLATER (127 D2) (*Ø L8*)
This small Victorian village (population of 1500) lies 66km/41mi west of Aberdeen in the shadow of the Lochnagar Mountains. It has a close connection with the English royals as the Queen and her family spend their summer holidays at *Balmoral Castle* only 10km/6.2mi away. As many of the shops supply Balmoral Castle they carry the Royal Warrant. Tourists can visit the castle, which is a fine example of Scots Baronial architecture, from May to July *(daily 10am–5pm | £8.50 | www.balmoral castle.com)*. The perfect place to stay is ● *Darroch Learg* country hotel and restaurant, a picture-perfect establishment tucked away on a green hill. The comfortable, cosy rooms have four poster beds

and are decorated in tartan prints. The restaurant serves exquisite cuisine using local, seasonal produce *(12 rooms | Ballater (A 93) | tel. 01339 75 54 | www.darrochlearg. co.uk | Moderate)*.

BRAEMAR (126 C2) (*Ø K8*)
The village is known for the *Highland Games* that take place on the first Saturday in September. Even the Queen, accompanied by the royal household, attends this traditional sports event that attracts some 20,000 spectators who descend on the tiny village (pop. 1200) annually. To avoid

⭐ **Ben Nevis**
A magnet for hikers and climbers determined to summit Scotland's highest peak → p. 66

⭐ **Glencoe**
A visit to the 'Valley of Tears' is an unforgettable outdoor experience → p. 67

⭐ **Cawdor Castle**
Shakespeare's Macbeth put this beautiful castle on the map → p. 69

⭐ **Loch Ness**
As mysterious as the myths surrounding its most famous inhabitant: Nessie → p. 70

⭐ **Loch Lomond**
Scotland's largest as most popular loch is where folk hero Rob Roy hid from the enemy → p. 71

⭐ **Fife**
A peninsula with charming villages → p. 73

MARCO POLO HIGHLIGHTS

disappointment it is best to book early in the year *(tel. 0845 2255121 *)*. *85km/ 52.8mi west of Aberdeen*

CAIRNGORMS NATIONAL PARK
(126–127 C–D 1–2) *(⌂ K 7–8)*

Great Britain's largest national park protects a quarter of the remaining Scottish forests and woodlands and many of its endangered plant species and wildlife. Balmoral Castle lies within its borders making it a favourite Royal Family holiday destination. Dominating the park are the 1300m/4265ft *Grampian Mountains*. A mountain road (A 939) wends its way through the barren, windy heights leading up to the Lecht ski resort *(www.lecht. co.uk)*. The park is popular with outdoor enthusiasts for its hiking and mountain bike trails (old paths once used by cattle drovers) as well as white river rafting (from Aviemore).

The River Dee, which flows into the sea at Aberdeen, has its source in the mountains here and *Royal Deeside* is what the Scots call the upper river valley. It encompasses the Balmoral estate where the royal family takes its Highland vacation from August to October. If you take a walk in the park around that time could even bump into nobility. You can join a Land Rover tour of the royal estate which gives visitors an idea of the efforts being made to boost the diminishing numbers of the magnificent Scottish pine. If you want to delve deeper into the secrets of Royal Deeside you should join the top rate tour that Ian Murray conducts *(www.lochnagar.net)*. He has documented the history of the area in three books and shares his wealth of knowledge with great enthusiasm on his walking tours.

In addition to the historical tour, you can join a INSIDER TIP four-wheel drive through the mountains between Braemar and Ballater with former policeman Neil Bain *(www.braemarsafaris.co.uk)*. Even if you don't spot an eagle, deer or grouse; you will be entertained by his repertoire of funny anecdotes about the local farmers and whisky distillers. *www.cairngorms. co.uk*

CRATHES CASTLE (127 E2) *(⌂ M8)*

Set in lush, landscaped gardens this is one of the most beautiful of Scotland's tower houses with magnificent interiors embellished with ceiling frescoes, antiques and one of the first holographs. The picture of a stag on the first floor ingeniously turns into a ship when you view it from the side *(daily 10.30am–5pm | £10 | Banchory). 25km/15.5mi west of Aberdeen*

DUNNOTTAR CASTLE (127 F2) *(⌂ M8)*

A dramatic and majestic castle ruin perched on a cliff overlooking the sea. A hiking trail leads up to it from the quaint, seaside town of Stonehaven. *Oct–April daily 10am–5pm | £5 | www.dunnottarcastle. co.uk | 25km/15.5mi west of Aberdeen*

FORT WILLIAM

(125 E3) *(⌂ G10)* **If you are expecting a romantic Highlands town, Fort William may come as a disappointment.**

The small town (pop. 4300), in the shadow of Ben Nevis, mainly serves as a transport hub and transit station for tours to the Highlands. The town was established as a fortification in 1655 and has a pedestrian zone that runs through it.

SIGHTSEEING

BEN NEVIS ★

The easy (but steep) hike up Great Britain's highest mountain (1344 m/4409ft) is what draws visitors to Fort William in the summer *(weather info: www.bennevis weather.co.uk)*. At the foot of the mountain the Nevis meanders through the *Glen Nevis* valley, popular among mountain bikers, hikers and climbers for its steep cliffs, waterfalls and the wild, scenic countryside. The landscape looks like something straight out of a film, so it comes as no surprise that it was the backdrop of choice for heroic epics such as 'Braveheart' and 'Rob Roy'. Experienced hikers will take a day or two to reach *Corrour Station* in Rannoch Moor *(32km/20mi from Fort William)*. A welcome sight as the Glasgow–Fort William line stops here on demand. 2km/1.2mi from the tiny train station building, on the fabulously beautiful *Loch Ossian*, is a ☺ INSIDER TIP youth hostel *(Budget)* – off the grid and entirely reliant on wind and solar energy. *www.glen-nevis.co.uk*

FOOD & DRINK

CRANNOG AT THE WATERFRONT
One of your best options for fresh seafood. *Daily | The Underwater Centre | tel. 01397 70 55 89 | www.crannog.net | Moderate*

WHERE TO STAY

THE LIME TREE
An art gallery, an excellent restaurant and a small, newly renovated hotel all in one. *9 rooms | The Old Manse | Achintore Road | tel. 01397 70 18 06 | www.limetreefort william.co.uk | Moderate–Expensive*

INFORMATION

FORT WILLIAM TOURIST BOARD
Cameron Square | tel. 01397 70 37 81 | www. visit-fortwilliam.co.uk; www.lochaber.com

WHERE TO GO

GLENCOE ★ (125 E3) (*Ø H10*)
Steep and brooding cliff walls rise up on either side of the dramatic Glencoe Gorge which becomes more isolated and rugged as it leads up into the narrow valley. Also known as the 'Valley of Tears' it gets its name from a massacre that took place on 13 February 1692. The MacDonald clan

Scotland's highest and most imposing mountain: Ben Nevis near Fort William chief was slow in pledging his oath of allegiance to King William of Orange. Wanting to set an example, the king used the Campbell's clan chief to carry out his plan. The latter stayed as an unsuspecting guest of the MacDonalds and during the night he and his men slaughtered the entire clan. This gruesome event is documented at the *Glencoe Visitor Centre.* Also plenty information about the valley's hiking trails *(daily 10am–5pm | www.glencoe-scotland.net). 30km/18mi south of Fort William*

INVERNESS

(130 A6) *(🗺 J 10)* **This lively city (pop. 46,000) is the primary city and shopping centre of the Highlands as well as being the hub for Highland and island tours.** Capital of the Highlands, its landmark is the *Caledonian Canal* which joins the west coast with the east coast and saves ships having to circumnavigate Scotland's northern tip. The picturesque canal is also popular with houseboats and narrowboats and stretches over 90km/60mi with 29 locks.

SIGHTSEEING

RIVER NESS
This is where you should come if you are looking for some peace and quiet. Take a walk or a cycle along its riverbanks. The path takes you past suspension bridges towards the northern end of the Caledonian Canal. From Inverness to Fort William it is a stretch of 100km/62mi through the *Great Glen* with brilliant views of the canal along the way and of the Highland mountains on the horizon.

FOOD & DRINK

ABSTRACT
Fine dining at its best: start off with a seven-course tasting menu then try one of the 250 malts in the piano bar. Then you can tumble straight into bed as the restaurant forms part of the stylish Glenmoriston Hotel *(30 rooms). 20 Ness Bank | tel. 01463*

Ships in the Caledonian Canal which connects the North Sea to the Atlantic

22 37 77 | www.glenmoristontownhouse. com | Moderate–Expensive

THE RIVERHOUSE RESTAURANT
Small and popular with the locals. *Closed Mon | 1 Greig Street | tel. 01463 22 20 33 | Moderate*

WHERE TO STAY

MELNESS GUEST HOUSE
Modern rooms in a beautiful Victorian townhouse at Inverness Castle. Good breakfasts. *2 rooms | 8 Edinburgh Road | tel. 01463 22 09 63 | www.melnessie.co. uk | Budget*

INFORMATION

INVERNESS TOURIST OFFICE
Castle Wynd/Bridge Street | tel. 01463 23 43 53 | www.inverness-scotland.com

WHERE TO GO

INSIDER TIP ALLADALE LODGE ☺
(130 A4) (*m* J7)
Highlands deluxe: the lodge is set in a 23,000 acre private estate. The mountainous and isolated environment is great for excursions on foot, on horseback or by four-wheel drive vehicle – the lodge is also open to day visitors.

The lodge accommodation (*Expensive*) comprises of a charming manor house and a number of cottages. The owner is millionaire Paul Lister, whose long-term goal is to turn the Scottish nature reserve into the kind of game reserves similar to those in South Africa. To find out more about this wilderness area, visit the *Croick Church* nearby. Etched into its window panes are the farewells of the subsistence farmers who were driven off the land in May 1845. *www.alladale.com | 70km/43mi north of Inverness*

CAWDOR CASTLE ★ (130 B6) (*m* J7)
Its tower has stood here since 1372 and more than 200 years later, in 1606, William Shakespeare set his play 'Macbeth' in Cawdor Castle. In the play Macbeth belongs to the Campbell clan – and they are real – the Campbells of Cawdor have been living in the castle for 600 years but leave in the summer when paying visitors arrive to get a glimpse of what lies behind the castle's walls. There are a number of unique gardens, some are French inspired. *May–beginning Oct 10am–5pm | £8.30 | www.cawdorcastle.com | 22km/13.6mi northeast of Inverness*

CULLODEN BATTLEFIELD
(130 A6) (*m* J7)
In 1746 Britain's last great battle took place here. Bonnie Prince Charlie had some men on his side but was defeated on the Highlanders moor by the Duke of Cumberland. The *Visitor Centre* details the battle *(daily 9am–6pm). 7km/4.3mi east of Inverness*

FINDHORN COMMUNITY ☺
(130 B5) (*m* K6)
Findhorn is a small eco-community in the north-east of Scotland. The 300 or so residents of the remote village live in harmony with nature, produce their own food, buy and sell with their own currency and lead a simple life. 'Stop worrying' is what the road signs say. What started off in one caravan as a new age idea has since evolved into a spiritual community where everybody has a place and a role to play. There is a visitors' centre for day visitors and you can take a guided tour *(£5)*. For guests spending the night there is a nice B & B (*Budget*) but guests are welcome to become part of the community for a period of time. Findhorn's residents pass on their knowledge through workshops and talks – they range from

self-awareness to ways to reduce the carbon footprint. *Findhorn near Forres | tel. 01309 69 03 11 | www.findhorn.org | 54km/ 34mi north-east of Inverness*

GLEN AFFRIC 🌿 (125 E1) (*ɯ H7*)

This has to be one of the most scenic Highland valleys in Scotland and home to the last forest of ancient Caledonian pine. Glen Affric is what the Highlands looked like before deforestation. Many hiking trails begin from *Loch Affric* (parking available at the privately-run Affric Lodge) among them a circular hiking trail around the loch (15km/9mi). A must for hikers is *Dog Falls*, a dramatic waterfall in a gorge below the dam. *45km/28mi south-west of Inverness*

INSIDER TIP LEAULT FARM ● (126 B1) (*ɯ K8*)

Good news for Border collie fans: on Leault Farm you can watch the dogs at work herding sheep. *Kincraig near Aviemore, take the B 9152 exit | May–Oct Sun–Fri noon and 4pm, July/Aug every two hours 10am–4pm | tel. 01540 65 13 10 | www.leault workingsheepdogs.co.uk*

LOCH NESS ★ (125 F1) (*ɯ J7*)

It goes without saying that this lake south-west of Inverness has to be Scotland's

BOOKS & FILMS

▶ **Killing the Shadows** – an exciting thriller about a serial killer on the prowl. His prey: authors of crime novels. Written by popular author Val McDermid.

▶ **The Falls: an Inspector Rebus Novel** – Edinburgh police detective John Rebus investigates a series of murders. The bodies of young women are found with a clue: a miniature coffin. Ian Rankin's dark and moody crime thrillers have attained cult status.

▶ **The Strange Case of Dr Jekyll and Mr Hyde** – in his 1886 novel Robert Louis Stevenson indirectly criticises the hypocrisy of the Victorian era, its respectable outward appearance belying dark desires.

▶ **For the Islands I Sing** – the autobiography of Scottish author George Mackay Brown is also an introduction to the magic of the Orkney Islands, his lifelong home and inspiration.

▶ **Local Hero** – an oil company wants to purchase a small Scottish village, and the surrounding countryside, to make way for a new refinery and sends in Burt Lancaster. He soon succumbs to the charms of the simple life. This comedy-drama, directed by Bill Forsyth and released in 1982, is a real gem.

▶ **Braveheart** – Mel Gibson directs and stars in this 1995 Oscar-winning historical epic based on the life of Scottish national hero, William Wallace.

▶ **Rob Roy** – this 1995 film based on the story of Robert Roy MacGregor (played by Liam Neeson) has some historical inaccuracies in its account of the story of Scotland's Robin Hood.

▶ **Trainspotting** – film director Danny Boyle's 1996 film is based on author Irvine Welch's novel about Edinburgh's chaotic drug scene.

most beautiful. It is 36km/22mi long and 1.5km/0.9mi wide and unusually deep at 325m/1066ft. The Loch Ness monster is still suspected to be lurking in its depths *(also see Trips & Tours)* and the favourite lookout point for researchers is *Urquhart Castle* on the north-western shore near *Drumnadrochit* – a picturesque 12th century ruin. Drumnadrochit is also the centre of the 'Nessie' cult and has the best exhibition: *Loch Ness 2000 | Feb–May/Oct 9am–5.30pm, Jun/Sept 9am–6pm July/Aug 9am–6.30pm, Nov–Jan 10am–3.30pm | £6.50 | www.lochness.com*

STIRLING

(126 B6) *(ᗄ J12)* **Overlooking the town (pop. 30,000) perched on a 75m/245ft high volcanic rock is Stirling Castle. It was heavily fought over in the 12th century and fell into the hands of the English in 1296.**

Control of the castle meant control over the country: it was the junction for all the important north-south routes. The Scotsman William Wallace recaptured the bridge in the Battle of Stirling Bridge – but it was not long before it landed up in the hands of the enemy again. It was Robert the Bruce who would finally conquer Stirling Castle in 1314.

INSIDER TIP ► Ardlui ferry departure point – where a mooring buoy has to be hoisted for a ride. The ferry means you are spared the last hour along the lake's northern shore so you can get to the *Drover's Inn* at Inverarnan *(£3)* far quicker!

Nessie lookout point: Urquhart Castle ruins

SIGHTSEEING

LOCH LOMOND ★ (126 A6) *(ᗄ H12)*
Scotland's largest and most popular lake. Geologically the Highlands begin on its southern shore; streets and a railway line run along its western shore; while the ● *West Highland Way* hiking trail is on its eastern shore. The most superb scenery is on the section that includes Rob Roy's cave hideaway (signposted) between Rowardennan, Inversnaid and the tiny

NATIONAL WALLACE MONUMENT ⋇ (126 B5) *(ᗄ J12)*
The film 'Braveheart' introduced the whole world to the story of William Wallace. It was at Stirling Bridge, 2km/1.2mi south of Stirling, that the Scottish national hero fought his famous battle. The museum houses his sword and if you brave the 246 stair climb to the top of the 67m/219ft high tower you will be rewarded with the most spectacular view towards Bannockburn. *Daily 10.30am–4pm | £5*

STIRLING CASTLE (126 B5) *(₥ J12)*

Imposing, fortified castle where the baby Mary Queen of Scots was crowned in 1543. The castle itself is dedicated to an exhibition of Highland coats of arms and standard-bearer. *April–Sept 9.30am–6pm, Oct–March 9.30am–5pm | £9*

FOOD & DRINK

HERMANN'S

An Austrian chef uses the best Scottish ingredients for his classic strudels, schnitzel and salmon. Something a little different but delicious! *Daily | Mar Place House | tel. 01786 45 06 32 | Moderate*

LOW BUDGET

▶ The more remote the area, the friendlier the locals: *Applecross Inn* across from Raasay Island offers affordable accommodation, great views and inexpensive meals. *7 beds | Applecross | tel. 01520 74 42 62*

▶ *Chlachaig Inn* is the meeting place for international climbers. Sit around the fire and enjoy an inexpensive beer, generous portions of pub food and affordable good accommodation. *Daily | 5km/3mi from Glencoe village | tel. 01855 81 12 52*

▶ *Drover's Inn* is a favourite among hikers on the West Highland Way. The bar serves excellent pies and succulent lamb. Camping *(£6)* on the farm next door. *Daily | tel. 01301 70 42 34 | Inverarnan near Ardlui*

WHERE TO STAY

ADAMO HOTEL

No plush upholstery, no overstuffed sofas just surprisingly contemporary and stylish décor in this luxury boutique hotel in the quaint town of Bridge of Allan. *10 rooms | Bridge of Allan | tel. 01786 83 32 68 | www.adamohotels.com | Budget–Moderate*

GLENEAGLES ●
(126 C5) *(₥ K11)*

This world-famous luxury hotel, 20km/12.4mi north-east of Stirling, is set in acres of expansive parklands and includes the most renowned golf course. The championship greens were designed by leading British golf course architects and the spa area is exceptional. Guests can enjoy special Balinese and Indian therapies; the one to try is the synchronised four-handed Purva Karma massage – pricey at £245 but well worth it. *222 rooms | Auchterarder | Tayside | tel. 0800 3 89 37 37 | www.glen eagles.com | Expensive*

INFORMATION

TOURIST INFORMATION CENTRE

41 Dumbarton Road | Stirling | www.visit scottishheartlands.com

WHERE TO GO

BLAIR CASTLE
(126 B3) *(₥ K10)*

This castle's whimsical fairytale appearance dates back to 1869 when the seventh Duke of Atholl, who had a weakness for Baronial architecture, had the building refurbished. Today, valuable works of art, paintings and antiquities are exhibited in its 32 rooms. *Daily 9.30am–5.30pm | £6.75 | www.blair-castle.co.uk | 100km/62mi north of Stirling*

The St Andrews cathedral ruin towers over the Fife coastline

DUNDEE (127 D4) (*L11*)

Scotland's fourth largest city (pop. 175,000) has an ancient city gate that dates back to 1519. It is also known in history as the city where the 'Discovery' was built. The ship that Robert Scott sailed in his expedition to the Antarctic in 1912. The ship is on display on the Discovery Quay *(Mon–Sat 10am–5pm, Sun 11am–5pm | £6). 85km/52.8mi north-east of Stirling*

FIFE ★ (127 D–E5) (*L 11–12*)

The lovely Fife peninsula is where Daniel Defoe invented his character, Robinson Crusoe, and it is also home to *St Andrews* – Great Britain's most exclusive golf club. The small town (pop. 14,000) revolves around golf and the University of St Andrews, Scotland's oldest university, where Prince William studied.

The jewel of the coastal towns is **INSIDER TIP** *Crail*, a charming, old harbour that is so picturesque that it has inspired many artists. Connoisseurs rate the *The Peat Inn* among the finest restaurant in Great Britain *(8 rooms | Cupar | tel. 01334 84 02 06 | www. thepeatinn.co.uk | Expensive). 60km/37mi east of Stirling*

PERTH (126 C5) (*K11*)

Perth was the capital of Scotland until 1452 and favoured, thanks to its ideal location on the River Tay, as a centre for wool and salmon. Today Perth (pop. 45,000) makes for an excellent springboard from which to set out for the Fife peninsula in the south-east, Stirling in the south-west or the Highlands in the north. *63 Tay Street* serves sumptuous Scottish-European cuisine. *(Closed Mon | tel. 01738 44 14 51 | Moderate)*.

On the outskirts is *Scone Palace*, famous for the *Stone of Scone,* a sandstone rock on which Scottish kings were enthroned. In the 9th century the then King of the Scots, Kenneth MacAlpin, brought the stone, which is now displayed at Edinburgh Castle, to Perth. Scone Palace has exhibits that include tapestries, paintings and ivory treasures *(April–Oct daily 9.30am–5pm | £5 | www.scone-palace.co.uk). 50km/31mi north-east of Stirling*

SCOTLAND AND ITS WHISKY

From its humble beginnings some 500 years ago *uisge neatha* – which means 'water of life', later shortened to *whisky* – has grown into one of Scotland's major exports. The most famous Scotch is single malt which is produced in a single distillery from a mash barley, water and yeast. The steps the barley undergoes from the field to the bottle can be quite involved. First the barley germinates, and then the germination process is halted by a heating process. The fire used in the drying process is often fed with sods of peat which gives many malt whiskies their distinctive, smoky taste. In the next stage the grain is crushed and mixed with locally sourced water. The barley malt separates into a sweet broth and grain waste – farmers use the waste as cattle feed – then yeast is added to ensure fermentation, and an alcoholic mash is created in the fermentation barrels. This preliminary stage whisky is then distilled in copper kettles in a complex double burning process. In this process, the middle distillate is mainly used because the pre and post flow is unpalatable.

The whisky then gets its golden colour from storage in oak barrels previously used to mature sherry or bourbon. The whisky must remain sealed in the barrels for three years under HM Customs and Excise supervision in order for it to be called whisky. A further few years will ensure that aromas are drawn from the barrels. Scotland's more than 800 whiskies get their unique flavours from a combination of the shape of the individual stills, the wood used for the barrels and even the environment. During the storage process some of the whisky will evaporate, and this percentage is known as the 'the angels' share' but the barrels also absorb the flavours of sea water or sea air.

FROM MALTS TO BLENDS

Scottish whisky is divided into three major groups. Firstly there is grain whisky, which is predominantly used as a mix for blended whiskies – whiskies blended to a uniform (brand) taste without any unwarranted surprises – and then there is malt whisky and malts are responsible for Scotland's reputation as a whisky nation. While single malts came from a single distillery, the traditional Scotch malts are usually mixed

Scotland's elixir of life: everything you need to know about the drying, fermentation and distillation process

blends. At the bottling stage water is added to the whisky to dilute it. Scotch has 40 per cent alcohol, other whiskies up to 46 per cent. Then there is the upper premium category of 'cask strength' whisky which is an acquired taste. This whisky is bottled at 50 per cent alcohol, tastes more intensive, and is also more expensive.

The tours on Islay and Orkney (at the Highland Park), as well as Arran – which has only had an operational distillery since 1995 – are particularly well presented. Shetland has the country's youngest distillery; it was launched in 2004 so the first ten-year-old whisky can be expected in 2014.

DISTINCTIVE DISTILLERIES

There are more than 100 active distilleries in Scotland. If you're after that distinctive smoky taste head to Islay with its nine distilleries (www.islaywhiskysociety.com) or in the east Highlands you can drive along the ★● Malt Whisky Trail (www.maltwhisky trail.com). The trail's tasting and nosing sessions make it a feast for the senses and you'll learn some fascinating details such as the fact that Glenvilet and Cardhu whiskies taste of heather rather than peat.

TIPS & TRICKS

Some restaurants also jump on the whisky bandwagon by offering dinners where a different malt whisky is served with every course.. A feat to get through even for a whisky-resilient Scotsman!

And how should whisky be taken? Neat or with a dash of water? It has been proven that a malt whisky releases the most flavours and aromas when served at room temperature with a dash of soft water added to it. *Slàinte!* Cheers!

THE WEST COAST & HEBRIDES

Hav bred ey (the islands at the edge of the sea) was the term the Vikings used for the Hebrides. The Inner Hebrides are clearly visible from the mainland.

While the Outer Hebrides lie far out in the Atlantic: a barren yet austerely beautiful paradise where tweed is woven and seals frolic in the bays and coves. Skye, the largest of the islands, is like a miniature version of Scotland. Small towns like Oban and Ullapool are ideal points from where to set out with your car, for a day trip with the ferry or a ride along the lonely western coastline. Those who visit the west coast and the islands are bound to fall in love with them.

OUTER HEBRIDES

(128 A–C 1–4) (𝄽 C–F 4–8) **The two islands of Lewis and Harris are connected by a narrow isthmus, both have a very Gaelic feel about them. Reasonable ferry prices and newly built accommodation have contributed to a small tourism boom.**

If you're heading for Lewis, its capital Stornoway (pop. 8000), is surprisingly urban while Harris has a landscape of contrasts. Its craggy rock-lined shores

Photo: Callanish Standing Stones

Highlands and islands: anyone who has visited the wild, dramatic west coast always returns again and again

reach up 700m/2300ft and the sea is the colour of the Caribbean. North and South Uist are enchanted islands with plenty of lakes.

SIGHTSEEING

BARRA (133 D5–6) (*ω C–D8*)

This island is synonymous with endless, sandy beaches, high mountain peaks, pre-historic ruins and Gaelic culture. *Castlebay* is its main town with its 13th century *Kisimul Castle*, which belongs to the MacNeil clan. Return ferries from the mainland leave from Mallaig and Oban. A unique phe-nomenon is Barra's tide-dependent flight connection to Glasgow. The Twin Otter aircraft uses the beach as a runway at low tide and in stormy conditions the island is completely cut off from the world by any

Hebridean solitude: one of many isolated bays that the Golden Road on Harris passes

transport *(www.flybe.com)* as no planes or ferries operate.

CALLANISH STANDING STONES ★ ●
(120 A2) *(ꕔ E4)*

This 5000 year old place of worship on Lewis consists of 50 standing stones laid out in the shape of a cross around what may once have been a tomb. Its full magic unfolds at INSIDERTIP sunrise when, with a little luck, you could have the site all to yourself.

GOLDEN ROAD ★ ☼
(128 A4) *(ꕔ E6)*

This single track tarmac road winds through the evocative, rocky landscape of Harris dotted with tweed weavers cottages and isolated bays. The road gets its ironic name from the enormous cost of building it. Take the detour through the moors between Finsbay (for its seals) and Leverburgh (the ferry). Drop in at the lovely INSIDERTIP *Skoon Art Café (Tue–Sat 10am–4.30pm | Budget)* in *Geocrab* for tea and cakes or a hearty bowl of soup.

INSIDERTIP ST KILDA (0) *(ꕔ B 5–6)*

When you try to locate St Kilda on a map you cannot help asking: did people live here? The archipelago lies some 80km/50mi west of Harris and is a remote collection of rock outcrops in the vast expanse of the Atlantic Ocean. Ever since the Neolithic era, people have tried to settle on St Kilda. Even the Vikings tried but no civilisation has managed to live here permanently. In 1930 the last 36 islanders moved to the mainland leaving behind the wind, the feral sheep and legions of seabirds. Today the entire group of islands around the main island of Hirta is the property of the National Trust of Scotland, a Unesco World Heritage Site and one of Europe's most important bird sanctuaries. A trip to these Scottish outposts is unforgettable: basking sharks and whales cavort in the Atlantic, and puffins and Soay sheep cling to the steep cliffs above the coastlines. Abandoned houses and crumbling church ruins bear testimony to attempts to make the rough land habitable. A day trip (three hours travelling time each way and a six-hour walking tour on land) is very manageable from Leverburgh on South Harris. Motorboats with room for twelve passengers do the trip out to St Kilda. *From £190| www.kildacruises.co.uk*

UIST ISLANDS (133 E3–5) *(⏉ D 6–8)*
The islands of North Uist, Benbecula and South Uist are joined to one another by causeways. Motorists set out for Uist from Leverburgh on Harris or from Skye on Scotland's west coast. Benbecula has an airport. The islands are ideal for birdwatching and the *Balranald Nature Reserve* on North Uist is a bird sanctuary with 183 species among them oystercatchers and plovers. In the east of the island, the village of *Lochmaddy* offers kayaking, diving and rock climbing *(tel. 01876 50 04 80 | www.uistoutdoorcentre.co.uk)*.
The western coast of South Uist has a 40km/24mi long beach covered in shells, set against a backdrop of dunes and wild flowers while the eastern coast is rugged and interspersed with lakes.

FOOD & DRINK

INSIDER TIP ▶ SCARISTA HOUSE
(128 A4) *(⏉ D6)*
This very homely restaurant is first rate when it comes to the preparation of local products such as lamb and langoustines. Scarista House is part of a country house hotel *(5 rooms/cottage | Moderate)* with beautiful beach and mountain views. *Closed Jan and Feb | tel. 01856 55 02 38 | www.scaristahouse.com | Moderate*

BEACHES

SCARISTA BEACH (128 A4) *(⏉ D6)*
This golden, fine sandy beach in western Harris is so beautiful and so romantic that some couples have tied the knot on it. To get there take the main road from Tarbert

in the direction of Rodel. You'll see the beach after 15km/9mi. There are no kiosks for snacks so it is best to take a picnic basket, two glasses and a bottle of your favourite tipple and watch the sun go down.

WHERE TO STAY

INSIDER TIP BLUE REEF COTTAGES ● ☺
(128 A4) *(⏉ D6)*
Two unique, turf roofed stone cottages in the breathtaking coastal beauty of Harris. For a whole week you can enjoy the stunning panoramic views from the huge picture windows – the tides, the eagles, the clouds drifting by and the magnificent sunsets. The hosts run their establishment with the kind of sustainable luxury that is also evident in the thousands of trees they have planted to offset the carbon footprint. You'll find a welcome bottle of champagne and fair trade goods in the luxury kitchen. *Scarista, Harris | tel. 01859 55 03 70 | www.stay-hebrides.com | Expensive*

⭐ **Callanish Standing Stones**
A mystery to this day: 50 giant stones jutting out into the landscape → p. 78

⭐ **Golden Road**
Take a drive on one of the world's most scenic roads → p. 78

⭐ **Trotternish Peninsula**
The Isle of Skye with its awe-inspiring coastline and massive mystical rock → p. 81

⭐ **Staffa**
Uninhabited and bizarre: the island off Mull is a natural wonder → p. 83

MARCO POLO HIGHLIGHTS

(128 B2) (*ɯ F4*)

This new guest house on the beach offers elegant and tasteful luxury. The décor in the rooms is contemporary and the excellent three course meals, prepared by the passionate chef (*Moderate*), are accompanied by wonderful sea views. *4 rooms | Back, Lewis | tel. 01851 82 09 90 | www. broadbayhouse.co.uk | Expensive*

HOTEL HEBRIDES
(128 A4) (*ɯ E5*)

Modern with a boutique hotel feel to it located in the North Harris ferry port. Both the bar and restaurant are surprisingly cool. Superb local cuisine! *21 rooms | Pier Road | Tarbert, Harris | tel. 01859 50 23 64 | www.hotel-hebrides.com | Moderate*

GEARRANNAN VILLAGE
(128 A2) (*ɯ E4*)

The rustle of the thatch and smoke rising from the chimney of these restored cottages gives you a real feel for what it must have been like to live in a blackhouse crofting village. You will experience history when you spend the night in Carloway where an old seaside village has been restored and turned into self-catering accommodation. *4 cottages | Carloway, Lewis | tel. 01851 64 34 16 | www.gearrannan.com | Moderate–Expensive*

LOCHMADDY HOTEL
(128 A5) (*ɯ D6*)

An established hotel, with the cosy charm of a historical house, it is located near the ferry terminal, the Centre for Gaelic Culture (*www.taigh-chearsabhagh.org*) and an outdoor centre. Nice rooms, good meals and a range of INSIDER TIP single rooms. *15 rooms | Lochmaddy, North Uist | tel. 01876 50 03 31 | www.lochmaddyhotel.co.uk | Budget–Moderate*

INFORMATION

TOURIST INFORMATION CENTRE
(128 B2) (*ɯ F4*)

26 Cromwell Street | Stornoway, Lewis | tel. 01851 70 30 88 | www.visithebrides.com

FERRIES

Operator for the ferry service from the mainland to the islands is *Caledonian MacBrayne*. Information: *tel. 0800 0 66 50 00 or www.calmac.co.uk*. For island hopping it is best to get the *Hebridean Hopscotch* ticket.

INNER HEBRIDES/ SKYE

(128 A–C 5–6) (*ɯ E–F 6–8*) **The Isle of Skye's (pop. 9500) name is from the Norse word *skuy* which means 'clouds and mist' and refers to the mist which sometimes shrouds the island.**

The diverse beauty of the island includes the dramatic *Cuillin* massif which is often covered in clouds. *Portree* is the picturesque main town in the east. Now that Skye is connected to the mainland by bridge, it is the only area of the Highlands and Islands that has recorded a rise in population figures.

SIGHTSEEING

CUILLINS (124 B–C1) (*ɯ F7–8*)

The town of Sligachan, in the middle of the island, serves as a departure point for tours to the *Red Cuillin*. These are more easily accessible than the *Black Cuillin*, where the highest mountain, *Sgurr Alasdair*, is 993m/3257ft high. Hardy swimmers can make their way to the icy INSIDER TIP *fairy pools* at the foot of the looming Black Cuillin mountain range. A truly magical, secret spot to swim is where the small road to Glenbrittle turns off to the north to the Glenbrittle valley.

DUNVEGAN CASTLE
(128 B6) (*ill E7*)
A rather quirky collection of items are on display in the austere-looking castle, among them is a lock of Bonnie Prince Charlie's hair. He hid in the castle after losing a battle on Skye. *March–Oct daily 10am–5pm | £5 | www.dunvegancastle.com*

TROTTERNISH PENINSULA ★
(128 B–C5) (*ill F6*)
A mystical rock, the *Old Man of Storr*, towers 45m/147ft above a picture-perfect coastline. At Staffin you can see how the rock was torn apart some 50 million years ago causing columns of 'pleats' in the aptly named *Kilt Rock*. At the northern end of the peninsula are the jagged *Quirang* rock formations that are often seen in car commercials.

FOOD & DRINK WHERE TO STAY

HARBOUR VIEW
(128 C6) (*ill F7*)
A small bistro serving excellent seafood. Best to reserve a table! *Closed Mon | Bosville Terrace | Portree | tel. 01471 6120 69 | Moderate*

THREE CHIMNEYS RESTAURANT
(128 B6) (*ill E7*)
An award-winning restaurant in an old crofter's cottage, serving exquisite cuisine. Exclusive accommodation offered in six rooms if you want to stay on longer. *Daily | Colbost, Dunvegan | tel. 01470 5112 58 | www.threechimneys.co.uk | Expensive*

INFORMATION

TOURIST INFORMATION
(128 C5) (*ill F7*)
Bayfield House | Portree | tel. 01478 612137 | www.skye.co.uk

Bizarre rock on Skye: the 'Old Man of Storr'

PLOCKTON (129 D6) (*ffl G7*)

This picturesque town is straight out of a story book! Its mild climate is influenced by the warm Gulf Stream which is why the palm-like cabbage trees thrive here. Old fishing and farming cottages huddle around the bay – today they serve as shops and small hotels. Spend the night and enjoy a meal at the *Plockton Hotel*, where the sea comes rushing into the bay right in front of your window *(14 rooms | 41 Harbour Street | tel. 01599 54 42 74 | www. plocktonhotel.co.uk | Budget–Moderate)*. *100km/62mi south-east of Skye*

SMALL ISLES

(124 B–C 2–3) (*ffl E–F 9–10*)

The fishing harbour *Mallaig* is where the Calmac ferry service leaves from for the archipelago but if it's island hopping you're after it is best to take the 'Shearwater' from the small town of *Arisaig.* Its timetable makes it possible to spend hours wandering around an island before being picked up again. The island of *Rum* (National Trust) is a dramatic natural wonder which boasts *Kinloch Castle* museum. Tours of the castle are timed to coincide with the arrival of the boat and give visitors an insight into the lives led by the nouveau riche industrialists a century ago. The *Isle of Muck* (pop. 30) island is an agricultural community run by the McEwen family which, for more than a century, have been successful in enticing families to settle here with their children. *Eigg* (pop. 70) is dominated by a 400m/ 1312ft high cliff, where *Massacre Cave* bears testimony to a violent history. In later years *Eigg* was long neglected by its absentee landlords but the island's fate took a happy turn in 1997 when the local inhabitants used state lottery funds to purchase the island for themselves. *www.road-to-the-isles.org.uk | www.arisaig.co.uk*

OBAN

(125 D5) (*ffl G11*) **This sickle-shaped, small town (population 8000), is regarded as the gateway to the Hebrides, a bustling fishing port with hotels and restaurants.**

Its landmark is a replica of the Colosseum, called *MacCaig's Folly*, which John Stewart MacCaig had built in 1897.

SIGHTSEEING

OBAN DISTILLERY

A whisky with a hint of peat has been produced here since 1794. Tours available. *Closed Jan | Stafford Street | tel. 01631 57 20 04 | £6 | www.discovering-distilleries. com*

FOOD & DRINK

EE-USK

What's in a name? In Gaelic *ee usk* means fish, just what this chic seafood and wine bar on the new harbour waterfront does best. A variety of fresh fish and shellfish and French wines. *Daily | North Pier | tel. 01631 56 56 66 | Budget–Moderate*

WHERE TO STAY

THE MANOR HOUSE ☆

A 200 year old Georgian villa, with a great view over the bay and superb cuisine. *11 rooms | Gallanach Road | tel. 01631 56 20 87 | www.manorhouseoban.com | Moderate*

INFORMATION

OBAN TOURIST INFORMATION

Argyll Square | Argyll | Oban | tel. 01631 56 31 22 | www.oban.org.uk

FERRIES

From Oban you can catch a ferry to the Inner and Outer Hebrides. *Ferry Terminal | tel. 01475 650100 | www. calmac.co.uk*

WHERE TO GO

INVERARAY (125 E5) (*Ø G11*)

A picturesque village (population 800) on *Loch Fyne* with a Georgian castle *(www. inveraray-castle.com)* and prison museum dating back to 1820 *(www.inveraray-jail. co.uk)*. 65km/40mi south-east of Oban

ISLAY & JURA

(120 A–B 1–2) (*Ø E–F 13–14*)

Aside from six distilleries Islay (pop. 3500) is also home to the first whisky academy. Here you can learn more about whisky nosing and etiquette as well as about the kinds of food that go best with whisky *(www.islaywhiskysociety.com)*. A good accommodation option is the *Harbour Inn* in Bowmore, the island's capital *(7 rooms | Harbour Side | tel. 01496 810330 | www. harbour-inn.com | Moderate)*.

The trip from Islay (Port Askaig) to Jura only takes a few minutes. The island is sparsely populated, with just 200 inhabitants, but does have some 5000 red deer. What few people know is that in 1946–47 British author, George Orwell, completed his oppressive novel, '1984' while on the island. *South-west of Oban*

MULL

(124 B–C 4–5) (*Ø E–F 10–11*)

The third largest Hebridean island is a haven for mountain hikers, offering picturesque seascapes. *Tobermory's* colourful houses extend around the bay. On the east coast is the Victorian-style *Torosay Castle* and its magnificent garden. *Daily 10.30am–5.30pm | west of Oban*

STAFFA ★ (124 B4) (*Ø E11*)

This small, bizarre, uninhabited island off the western coast of Mull owes its popularity to its unique basalt volcanic formations. The hall-like *Fingal's Cave*, where

A marvel of nature: the basalt pillars of the Hebridean island of Staffa

the waves produce haunting sounds, inspired Felix Mendelsohn's overture 'The Hebrides'. Boats to the island leave from Iona and Fionnphort on Mull (daily | £20 | www.staffatrips.f9.co.uk). You can only disembark in good weather.

TIREE AND COLL

(124 A–B 3–4) (*m̈* D–E 10–11)
These two islands, between the Inner and Outer Hebrides, offer the most hours of sunshine and are idyllically secluded. They epitomise the true desert island setting – dunes and white sandy beaches. Tiree (pop. 760) is a windsurfer paradise and hosts an international surf festival in October while Coll (pop. 150) is scattered with Stone Age relics. Both islands have cosy hotels that offer full board and lodging and excellent seafood (Scarinish Hotel | Tiree | tel. 01879 2 20 03 08 | Budget and Coll Hotel | tel. 01879 23 03 34 | Budget). To get there take a ferry (www.calmac.

co.uk) or a light aircraft (www.hebridean air.co.uk) from Oban.

ULLAPOOL

(129 E4) (*m̈* G6) **Colourful houses are gathered around the harbour of quaint Ullapool (pop. 1200) which is a bustling tourist town that becomes a hotspot for tourists in the summer.**
It is from here that the ferries depart to Lewis and Harris in the Outer Hebrides, and from here there are excursions to the *Summer Isles*, a group of small islands where you can watch seals, dolphins and birds (tours operated by MV 'Summer Queen' | tel. 01854 61 24 72).

FOOD & DRINK WHERE TO STAY

THE ALBANNACH
In *Lochinver*, where mountains and coastline are scenic and dramatic, The Albannach offers individually decorated rooms and suites and guests (and non-residents) can also book a dinner table in their Michelin star restaurant (Moderate–Expensive). 5 rooms | Lochinver | 15km/9mi north of Ullapool | tel. 01571 84 44 07 | www.the albannach.co.uk | Moderate–Expensive

INSIDER TIP THE CEILIDH PLACE ●
This establishment feels like a home away from home: cosy restaurant (Moderate), a wonderful book store, charming hotel and inviting hostel all in one. 13 rooms | 14 West Argyle St | tel. 01854 61 21 03 | www. theceilidhplace.com | Budget–Moderate

INFORMATION

TOURIST OFFICE
6 Argyle Street | tel. 01854 612135 | ullapool@host.co.uk

LOW BUDGET

▶ The *Gatliff Trust Hotels* are four rustic and inexpensive accommodation options in the Outer Hebrides (in Garenin, Rhenigidale, Berneray and Howmore) for backpackers. Locals now run the old traditional croft-houses, once inhabited by farmers, as hostels. Peat fires and showers: www.gatliff.org.uk

▶ The *Caledonian MacBrayne* shipping company offers an Island Rover ticket that permits you to visit as many islands as you like in 8 (£50) or 15 (£75) days. Motor cars from £235, bicycles free of charge. tel. 0800 06 50 00 | www.calmac.co.uk

THE WEST COAST & HEBRIDES

Fishermen carefully preparing their nets in Ullapool's harbour

WHERE TO GO

CAPE WRATH (129 E1) (*H3*)

Take either the ferry or the minibus from *Durness* to the cliffs and the lighthouse *(daily May–Sept)* or go on a hike along the challenging but breathtaking 28km/17mi coastline between the Cape and *Kinlochbervie*. *www.capewarth.org.uk | 70km/43mi north of Ullapool*

HANDA ISLAND (129 E2) (*G–H 4*)

The boat trip to the bird island takes 30 minutes from the remote Tarbet Pier north of Scourie. A 2.5km/1.5mi walk ends with a 350m/1148ft high cliff densely populated with seabirds and if you scramble over the rock along the coast, you'll get pretty close to the seals. Highly recommended: round off your trip with a visit to the castle in Tarbet and enjoy a seafood meal afterwards at the Shorehouse Café *(April–Sept, Mon–Sat, noon–8pm | Budget)*

INSIDER TIP INVEREWE GARDENS ●
(129 D4) (*G6*)

In 1862 when the Scotsman Osgood Mackenzie put a fence around three plants, he had no idea that this would result in one of the most northerly botanical gardens in the world. Located right by the sea, the Inverewe Gardens are divided into themed sections and is a paradise of exotic and subtropical plants. *Daily 9.30am–5pm | £7 | Poolewe | 80km/50mi south of Ullapool*

LOCHINVER
(129 E3) (*G5*)

This small village is a working fishing port, it feels like it is exposed to the Atlantic and unprotected from the elements, you reach it via a very winding and scenic coastal road. You may even spot porpoises in the bay in Lochinver, which is on the coast of the *Assynt* district with its great hiking trails. Guided tours will teach you about the geology, fauna and flora and history of the area. There are also some very deep caves in the area – Scotland's deepest is *Bone Cave* in the Assynt district – that sheltered people in prehistoric times. Completing the picture-perfect setting is the *Ardvrech Castle* fortress ruin on *Loch Assynt*. *www.assyntfoundation. org*

ORKNEY & SHETLAND

The Pentland Firth is a strait that separates the melancholy of the Highlands from the wide open pastures and beautiful, sandy beaches of Orkney.

Some 20,000 Orcadians engage in livestock farming and their relative wealth stems from the fact that during World War I they sold produce to the English based in the *Scapa Flow* inland sea. The farmers used the money earned to purchase their own farmland, releasing them from the land barons. Orkney's inhabitants are first and foremost farmers while the opposite is true for the Shetlanders, most of whom are in the fishing industry. Orkney, whose settlement goes back some 5000 years, is testimony to how its inhabitants made this remote northern region work for them. Shetland continues to draw visitors with its rustic charm, great diversity of bird life and the magical light display of the aurora borealis.

ORKNEY ISLANDS/ MAINLAND

(131 D–E 2–3) (*M K–M 1–3*) Good roads lead through the pastures past lochs on

Welcome to Orcadia: on the trail of seabirds, the Northern Lights and the Atlantic island way of life

the mostly flat peninsula that make up this rugged Orcadian archipelago.

Stretching out to a maximum of 35km/21mi by 20km/12mi is Mainland, the most important and largest of the islands in the archipelago. There are beaches right around the island and some magnificent cliffs on its western coast. On an isthmus between east and west Mainland is *Kirkwall* (pop. 6100), the bustling main

town with its harbour pier and beautiful sandstone cathedral. The small airport is only a few miles from Kirkwall.

SIGHTSEEING

ITALIAN CHAPEL ● ⋰
(131 E3) (*Ø* L3)

In 1943 Italian prisoners of war were deployed in Kirkwall to build concrete barriers between the islands to deter German submarines, while on the island they converted two Nissen huts into an a small but impressive chapel. The altarpiece depiction of the Madonna and Child was done using a Christmas card as a template. A touching building with lovely sea views. *7km/4.3m south of Kirkwall*

Skara Brae's Stone Age settlement

MAES HOWE (131 E2) (*L2*) ●

You have to crouch to get through the low passage to enter into this 5000 year old chamber tomb at Finstown. In the 12th century the Vikings probably used it to shelter from storms. They left behind some carved runic graffiti on the walls, the characters sing the praises of a certain 'beautiful Ingeborg', and today the inscriptions are used on jewellery made in Orkney. The magnificent tomb forms part of the so-called *Heart of Neolithic Orkney* Unesco World Heritage Site together with the Ring of Brodgar, Skara Brae and the Standing Stones of Stenness. *10km/6.2mi west of Kirkwall*

ORKNEY MUSEUM (131 E2) (*L2*)

In Tankerness House, opposite Kirkwall's cathedral, the museum documents the amazing 5000 year old history of Orkney. *Mon–Sat 10.30am–5pm (Oct–March closed 12.30pm–1.30pm.), May–Sept also Sun 2pm–5pm*

INSIDER TIP ▶ PIER ART CENTRE
(131 E3) (*L2*)

A great gallery for contemporary art, located on a pier in Stromness harbour. *Tue–Sat 10.30am–12.30pm and 1.30pm–5pm | Victoria Street | www.pierartcentre.com*

RING OF BRODGAR ★
(131 E2) (*L2*)

This phenomenal stone circle – comprising 27 (originally 60) 4.7m/15ft high stones – has a diameter of 104m/340ft and its size meant that it could have held some 3000 people at one time. When researchers tried to calculate how many hours of hard labour it would have taken our Neolithic ancestors to build the Ring of Brodgar they came to an astounding 80,000 working hours.
The remains of the *Standing Stones of Stenness* are visible from the Ring. *23km/14.2mi north-west of Kirkwall*

SKARA BRAE ★ (131 D2) (*L2*)

This is the best preserved Neolithic settlement in Europe: the ruins of the village on the west coast provide fascinating evidence of how people lived here 5000 years ago. In 1850 a storm stripped off the earth and uncovered the cluster of eight homes. *30km/18mi north-west of Kirkwall*

ST MAGNUS CATHEDRAL
(131 E2) (*L2*)

When this magnificent pink sandstone cathedral was built in 1137, it was still right by the sea. Today, it is in the middle of Kirkwall and is still one of the most beautiful churches in northern Europe.

STROMNESS (131 E3) (*L2*)

This former herring fishing harbour was where the North Sea expeditions took their drinking water on board. The small town (population 1800) has to be one of northern Scotland's most melancholy and poetic places. It has incredibly narrow alleys and you'll want to while away some time listing to live music in its pubs. Stromness is the perfect stepping stone to the enchanting Isle of Hoy (30 min by ferry) and for diving excursions in the *Scapa Flow*. Next to the campsite at the harbour is a ◣◣ INSIDER TIP golf course with fabulous views.

YESNABY SEA STACKS & MARWICK HEAD (131 D2) (*L2*)

These two dramatic cliffscapes on the north-western coast of Mainland attract hikers and birdwatchers from May to August to see the thousands of breeding seabirds (such as puffins, fulmars and skuas) up close.

FOOD & DRINK

CREEL INN & RESTAURANT
(131 E3) (*L3*)

A top-notch seafood restaurant and cosy country guest house (*3 rooms | Budget*). Reservations essential! *Jun–Aug. Closed Mon (entirely closed in winter) | about 8km/5mi south of Kirkwall | tel. 01856 83 13 11 | Moderate–Expensive*

JULIA'S CAFÉ (131 E3) (*L2*)

Pies, cakes and vegetarian food served from early till late, at Julia's everything is home-made. Popular with the locals. *Daily | Ferry Road | Stromness | tel. 01856 85 09 04 | Budget*

Beautiful interior of the Magnus Cathedral

MARCO POLO HIGHLIGHTS

⭐ **Ring of Brodgar**
In diameter larger than Stonehenge: the great stone circle is Orkney's mystical highlight → p. 88

⭐ **Skara Brae**
This well preserved Neolithic settlement remained buried under sand dunes for centuries → p. 88

⭐ **Hoy**
Orkney's second-largest island boasts huge colonies of puffins and a bizarre red sandstone coast → p. 91

⭐ **Mousa Broch**
Eerie and atmospheric in the evening: the Pictish round tower in a breathtaking setting → p. 92

SHOPPING

Mainland is a shopper's paradise for those after high-quality crafts that reflect the rich regional culture. The creations inspired by nature, or the Nordic and Celtic myths from its more than 5000 years of history, are not to be missed. The *Orkney Craft Trail (www.orkneydesignercrafts.com)* and the *Artist's Studio Trail (www.orkneyartstrail.co.uk)* leads you to individual studio addresses.

HIGHLAND PARK DISTILLERY
(131 E2) (*ɰ L2*)

Whisky has been proudly produced here for 300 years and the number of awards this distillery has won bear testimony to decades of excellence. The distillery upholds traditional techniques, which means that you can still observe the INSIDER TIP floor malting germination of the barley here to this day. *Tours daily 10am–4pm | Holm Road | Kirkwall | tel. 01856 87 46 19 | www.highlandpark.co.uk*

SPORTS & ACTIVITIES

INSIDER TIP **SCAPA FLOW DIVING**
Scapa Flow (131 E3) (*ɰ L2*) lies between the islands of Mainland, Hoy and South Ronaldsay and is almost like an inland sea. Right in the middle of it at a depth of between 26m/85ft and 4m/150ft are half a dozen sunken German warships from World War I. Excursions for experienced scuba divers start from Stromness. Information and equipment: *The Diving Cellar | 4 Victoria Street, Stromness | tel. 01856 85 03 95 | www.divescapaflow.co.uk*

WHERE TO STAY

AYRE HOTEL
(131 E2) (*ɰ L2*)

A dignified, country house atmosphere in the main town in Kirkwall: tea is served in the garden. *33 rooms | Ayre Road | Kirkwall | tel. 01856 87 30 01 | www.ayre hotel.co.uk | Expensive*

The Old Man of Hoy – a dramatic landmark on the second-largest of the Orkney Islands

STROMNESS HOTEL
(131 E3) *(∅ L2)*

Comfortable hotel in an historic building with cosy, traditional bar popular with locals. Ask for a room overlooking the working harbour. *42 rooms | Pier Head | Stromness | tel. 01856 85 02 98 | www. stromnesshotel.com | Moderate*

INFORMATION

TOURIST INFORMATION CENTRE
(131 E2) *(∅ L2)*

6 Broad Street | Kirkwall | tel. 01856 87 28 56 | www.visitorkney.com

ISLANDS IN THE AREA

HOY ★ (131 D–E3) *(∅ K–L 3)*

This is Orkney's second largest island and definitely warrants a visit. Hikers will enjoy the heather covered hills, Atlantic puffins and sandstone cliffs that glow red at sunset The scenic three-hour hike from the dramatic Rackwick Bay in the west to the fantastic rock spire, *Old Man of Hoy,* makes for an unforgettable experience. The ferry ride itself to and from Stromness/ Mainland *(two to three times daily)* is almost like a mini cruise *(tel. 01856 79 13 13).* Information: *Tourist Information Stromness (at the harbour) | www.hoyorkney.com*

INSIDER TIP NORTH RONALDSAY
(131 F1) *(∅ M1)*

As if symbolic of the life of a small isolated island community, a 21km/13mi long stone dyke surrounds this remote Orkney Island. It keeps the sheep away from the pastures and forces them towards a diet of kelp and seaweed in an area that is home to plenty of seals and seabirds. Worth the two-and-a-half hour cruise from Kirkwall for its stunning sandy beach, the wind and solar energy powered ☺ *Bird Observatory (www.nrbo.co.uk),* as well as the old stone lighthouse. Tip: spend the night on the island at the nature centre's *Observatory Hostel (10 beds | tel. 01857 63 32 00 | Moderate)* and then fly back by light aircraft *(www.loganair.co.uk)* afterwards – an INSIDER TIP amazing sightseeing adventure. Info: *Tourist Information Kirkwall | www.orkneyferries.co.uk*

PAPA WESTRAY ☺ (131 E1) *(∅ L1)*

This small (it is only 3.5 square miles), fair trade island is in the northern part of the archipelago, where the North Sea meets the Atlantic. The fair trade status was awarded to Papa Westray because everyone from the baker to the mayor upholds fair trade practices. Actually sustainability has been integral to the island for a long time now. Several years ago when the ferry service was to be discontinued, due to decline in use, the 70 or so islanders formed a cooperative to keep the crossings alive. In the interim the cooperative has also converted old farm buildings into hostels and hotel accommodation, opened a nature reserve and instigated a conservation drive to preserve the island's cultural heritage. Sites being protected are the well restored Neolithic home, the *Knap of Howar,* a 'hogback' or carved Viking gravestone dating back to the 12th century, the 17th century manor house on *Holland Farm* and the island museum. If you need some excitement after the peace and quiet of the island, you can consider leaving by plane. The world's shortest scheduled flight operates between Papa Westray and the larger island of Westray: it takes just two minutes! Once on Westray you should not miss the pride of the island: a small 5000 year old sandstone Neolithic figurine, the 'Orkney Venus', which was discovered in 2009. A year later archaeologists discovered a second figurine at the same site. *www.westray papawestray.co.uk*

SHETLAND ISLANDS/ MAINLAND

(132 B2–5) (_M B3_) The narrow and elongated Mainland, the largest of the Shetland Islands, is characterised by rugged bays and scenic fjords or _voes_.
Lerwick (pop. 7000) is the main town, most important harbour and heart of this windswept hilly island. The scenery here is like the Highlands in miniature with a number of beautiful, sandy beaches and a dramatic rocky coastline. To the south is the airport, the _Sumburgh Head_ cliff, the wreck of the stricken oil tanker 'Braer' and archaeological excavations. All the place names and geographical references reflect the Norse heritage from the Vikings who settled here in the 9th century. To this day Scotland's northernmost inhabitants still have a greater affinity for Norway than Edinburgh or London.

LOW BUDGET

▶ Great accommodation in an excellent location: _Hamnavoe Hostel_ is in a wonderfully atmospheric coastal village. _13 beds | tel. 01856 85 12 02 | 10a North End Road | Stromness_

▶ Self-catering Shetland on a shoestring: _Camping Böds_ are eight old fishmen's cottages. They are inexpensive and very basic and are all in great locations with an interesting history. _Take your own sleeping bag and camping stove. April–Sept | www.camping-bods.com_

SIGHTSEEING

JARLSHOF (132 B5) (_M B3_)
The showpiece of archaeological evidence of settlement in the North Atlantic, it takes you on a journey from the Stone and Bronze Ages, Picts and Viking eras, the Middle Ages to the modern era. _Sumburgh Head | April–Sept Mon–Sat 9.30am–6.30pm, Sun 2pm–6.30pm_

MOUSA BROCH ★
(132 B4) (_M B3_)
Brochs were the double-walled residential towers of the Picts and this one, standing 13m/42ft tall, is Scotland's mightiest. Located on the island of Mousa, it is shrouded in a eerie atmosphere at dusk when thousands of small, black storm petrels fly up from the rocky beach below it. _Ferry from Sandwick_

SCALLOWAY (132 B4) (_M B3_)
Distinctive for its 500 year old fortress ruin, silhouetted against the harbour backdrop, this was once the capital of the Shetland Islands – to view _Scalloway Castle_ you have to collect the key from the Royal Hotel. _Scalloway Museum_ details the role that the town played in World War II when Scalloway (pop. 1300) was the headquarters of the Norwegian resistance. This is where the so-called _Shetland Bus_ boat escape route to and from the Nazi occupied Norway was based. From 1940 thousands of Norwegians were rescued via the sea route – initially with fishing boats then later with some fast submarine chasers.

ST NINIAN'S ISLE
(132 B4) (_M B3_)
At low tide a golden sandy beach extends all the way to this offshore island where the remains of a church and a Celtic silver treasure have been found.

FOOD & DRINK

BUSTA HOUSE HOTEL
(132 B3) (*ØJ B3*)
A romantic country house hotel *(22 rooms | Moderate)* that combines history with hospitality. The finest cuisine on Shetland. *Daily | Brae | tel. 01806 52 25 06 | www. bustahouse.com | Moderate–Expensive*

MONTY'S BISTRO (132 B4) (*ØJ B3*)
The best place to eat in Lerwick: delicious home-made breads, seafood and puddings. *Daily | 5 Mounthooly Street | Lerwick | tel. 01595 69 65 55 | Moderate*

WHERE TO STAY

SUMBURGH HOTEL (132 B5) (*ØJ B3*)
A stay at this manor house is well worth it for the atmosphere and views, the excellent salmon and its proximity to the prehistoric site of Jarlshof and the spectacular cape, *Sumburgh Head*. *32 rooms | Sumburgh | tel. 01950 46 02 01 | www. sumburghhotel.com | Moderate*

INFORMATION

TOURIST INFORMATION CENTRE
(132 B4) (*ØJ B3*)
Market Cross | Lerwick | tel. 01595 69 34 34 | www.visitshetland.com

ISLANDS IN THE AREA

INSIDER TIP ▶ FAIR ISLE
(132 A–B6) (*ØJ B4*)
Britain's remotest inhabited island (population 70) has impressive 200m/656ft high cliffs and flocks of migratory birds. You can get there by excursion boat *(2.5 hours from Grutness/Sumburgh Airport)* or by plane *(from Tingwall, 25 minutes)*. There is also the option to overnight *(Moderate)*. *www.fairisle.org.uk*

Like father, like son – sheep farmer on the Shetlands

INSIDER TIP ▶ FOULA (132 A4) (*ØJ A3*)
This wild, deserted island (pop. 30) is home to millions of marine birds including some 3500 pairs of nesting skuas – they will even attack the islanders who are out peat cutting. The *Gaada Stack* is an imposing rock formation off the north coast. Accommodation is available at *Leraback Bed & Breakfast (tel. 01595 75 32 26 | marion@foula.net | Budget)*. Boats leave for Foula from Walls or Scalloway twice a week *(tel. 01595 84 08 80 | www.atlantic ferries.co.uk)* or you can catch a flight from Tingwall *(tel. 01595 84 02 46 | www.direct flight.co.uk)*.

UNST ☆ (132 C1) (*ØJ C1*)
One of the Shetland's most northerly points is here on the island: *Herma Ness*. The headland is haven for hikers with superb views over the bird-covered coast all the way to the lighthouse! Easily accessible by car via the roll-on roll-off ferry.

TRIPS & TOURS

The tours are marked in green in the road atlas, the pull-out map and on the back cover

1 THE SECRET OF LOCH NESS

The waters of Loch Ness cut sharply and deeply into the Highland landscape. Beneath its surface moves a secret that has captured the imagination of many for centuries: the Loch Ness monster. The loch is almost 38km/24mi long but is only about 1.5km/1mi wide. Herewith a suggested route for a one or two day trip by car. Round trip about 100km/62mi.

You can reach Drumnadrochit – the research capital for Nessie, the Loch Ness monster, on the northern shore – from Inverness → p. 68 via the A 82 where there are a handful of hotels, an award winning pub, a grocery store and two Nessie exhibitions. The more popular of the two may be more colourful but not necessarily better than *Loch Ness 2000 (Feb–May daily 9.30am–5pm, June/Sept 9am–6pm, July/Aug 9am–6.30pm | £6.50 | www.lochness.com)* arguably a more interesting take for the enquiring mind. The exhibition was conceptualised by Adrian Shine, who arrived at the loch 30 years ago to track down Nessie. Over the years he has become increasingly sceptical and makes a painstaking case for and against the existence of the monster.

From Loch Ness to Harry Potter: you need not travel far to be drawn in by the magic of Scotland

The monster was first spotted by an Irish missionary in 565. Ever since 1933, when the road around Loch Ness was expanded, the number of eye witness accounts has increased dramatically. Today up to 240,000 visitors a year make their way to the loch and boats equipped with video and sonar scout the lake daily.

If you want to join the search, George Edward will be all too pleased to take you into the dark, mysterious waters with his boat *(Loch Ness Cruises | tickets in advance tel. 01456 45 03 95 | 1 hour £10 | http:// loch-ness-cruises.co.uk)*.

All that detracts from the eerie lapping of the lake's waters against the hull is George belting out: 'Keep your cameras ready!'. The loch goes down to a depth of some 300m/984ft, a gigantic fresh-water basin that formed after the Ice Age, and is the perfect hideaway for an alien species.

● Steve Feltham calls himself a 'full-time Nessie hunter' and is based in the village of Dores on the eastern shore. Follow the

Mystery solved: Nessie is a cuddly toy

A 82 to Fort Augustus at the southern tip of the lake and drive along the east side towards Inverness. From Foyers the road takes you along the lake shore to Dores. On the shore below The Dores Inn is Steve Feltham's home, a camper van with a 'Nessie-Sery Independent Research' logo. He supports himself by making and selling small INSIDER TIP Nessie statues from colourful model clay for £7 a piece *(www. haveyouseenityet.co.uk)*.

Go on your own Nessie watch and make an advance booking with Evergreen B&B on the other side of the lake with its perfect loch views *(2 rooms | Inverfarigaig | tel. 01456 48 67 17 | www.evergreenlochness. co.uk | Moderate)*.

2 TWEED TOUR OF LEWIS AND HARRIS

A familiar sound on the Outer Hebrides islands of Harris and Lewis is the clatter of weaving looms. Harris Tweed has been manufactured here for centuries. Most of the weavers live along Harris' Golden Road, in a landscape reminiscent of the rolling green hills of Ireland. From the Highlands you can head to the islands by car and undertake a two day round trip once there. Round trip approx. 280km/173mi.

In season the *Caledonian MacBrayne (www. calmac.co.uk)* ferry transports passengers and vehicles from Ullapool to Stornoway on Lewis → p. 76, a port that is abuzz with fishing boats and seals vying for scraps. The trip takes two and a half hours and operates up to three times daily. The ferry now also operates on Sunday, the holy day for the island's staunchly Protestant community. The 19th century Lewis Castle is the small town's landmark. It was built by a Scotsman who made his fortune from the opium trade. Later it was bought and donated to Lewis by the philanthropist and Lever Brothers millionaire, Lord Leverhulme.

Start your trip around the island from Stornoway and head north on the B 895. After 10km/6.2mi you'll reach Broad Bay House → p. 80 offering lovely accommodation by the beach. A mile or so further on, shortly before the end of the road, are a few more endlessly long beaches. As the road ends here, make an about-turn and travel across Lewis on the A 857 in a westerly direction. At Barvas switch to the A 858 where you'll now drive along the coast towards Harris – with ⚓︎ the most beautiful views as a reward. In Arnol, a small community, is the original Blackhouse Museum *(April–Sept Mon–Sat*

9.30am–5.30pm, Oct–March Mon–Sat until 4.30pm | entrance £2.50) which shows the thatched farm cottages typical of the regional, where the open indoor fires cover the walls in soot – hence the term 'blackhouse'. 15km/9.3mi further down the coast is **Gearrannan Blackhouse Village → p. 80** – a completely preserved and renovated farming village by the sea, where you can spend the night. It's well worth the climb up the hill for the great view of the old fields and the beach where the boats would once moor – a sight typical of a traditional crofting village. Slightly further south is where you will find **Dun Carloway Broch**, the ruin of a 2000 year old tower house. The most mystical place you'll come across however has to be the **Callanish Standing Stones → p. 78**, an Anglo-Saxon place of worship that dates back 5000 years. It is made up of 48 stones laid out as a Celtic cross and may have been used for rituals relating to the sun or moon.

On the other side of Achmore, make a right turn into the A 859 towards Harris. At Tarbert you'll reach the beautiful neighbouring island of **Harris**. From here it is only 8km/5mi to the ☼ **Golden Road → p. 78**, a narrow road along the rugged east coast where the views of the sea through the granite hills are austere but breathtakingly beautiful. Every so often en route here you'll come across a tiny hamlet that seems entirely untouched by time, and where tweed looms still clatter. The highlight on this stretch is **Scarista beach → p. 79**, in the west of Harris, with its endless white sands and the pristine sea shimmering in shades of tourmaline.

Luskentyre's beach is crescent shaped and slides gently into the sea, the water is so clear here, you can see all the way to the bottom – the epitome of a perfect seascape. A row of eight houses and a cemetery by the sea are the only telltale signs that people also live here, and the locals here are as relaxed as their surroundings. This means you can even turn up unannounced at celebrated tweed weaver Donald John Mackay. He became world famous in 2005 when the sports brand Nike ordered miles of his tweed for a new range of sport shoe.

Rodel in the south of Harris is the most likely end to your tour where the small **St Clement's Church** has some sculptured

Harris has the most beautiful beaches

clan chief tombstones worth seeing. From Harris you can either drive back to Lewis or set out from Leverburgh to the Uist group of islands → p. 79 taking the ferry back to Mainland from Lochboisdale on South Uist.

3 SCOTLAND BY TRAIN

A train journey across Scotland combines both romantic and relaxation – the perfect way to take in the beautiful countryside at your leisure. The railway lines lead from Edinburgh and Glasgow all the way through moors and mountain valleys to the ferry for Orkney. Info: *www.scotlandrailways.com*

Waverley Station, all aboard! The name of Edinburgh's → p. 52 main train station was named after Walter Scott's 1841 historical novel. Trains depart here several times an hour on the 50 minute commute to Glasgow → p. 42, a metropolis that is completely different in character from Edinburgh. If you decide to spend a few days in Glasgow a great accommodation option is the trendy hotel *Citizen M (198 rooms | 60 Renfrew Street | www.citizen glasgow.com | Moderate)*.

The ● West Highland Line leaves Glasgow's main Queen Street station up to six times daily for Fort William, the small railway cars seemingly dwarfed by the increasing grandeur of the landscape. The final stops are Oban and Mallaig on the west coast. Initially the train follows the River Clyde with images of industrial activity gliding by. Next it heads north along the entire length of Loch Lomond → p. 71 rumbling its way through forests, with views of the lake. At Ardlui the train leaves the lake behind and soon reaches Crianlarich, where the railway line forks off to Oban in a westerly direction. The Oban stretch

travels through the western Highlands with its scenic mountains, rivers and lakes. The trip from Glasgow to Oban is a good three hours. Oban is a bustling coastal town with whisky distilleries and crossings to the Inner Hebridean islands of Mull, Islay and Jura. If you decide to stay on then the lovely Manor House Hotel → p. 82, with its view over the bay, is a good option.

However, if you decide instead to take the Fort William stretch, the train will take you along the West Highland Way → p. 71 which means it is also popular with hikers and for those too wary to hike. It continues along the West Highland Way as far as Bridge of Orchy where it leaves the trail and trundles across the austere wilderness of Rannoch Moor where the loneliest station in the country appears out of nowhere. Corrour Station → p. 67 is a request stop for hikers doing the moors on foot to Fort William or eastward to Dalwhinnie. A mile away is the Loch Ossian youth hostel, idyllically located right by the lake – the perfect stop for anyone seeking the peace and quiet of the great outdoors.

Fort William → p. 66, the destination for mountain bikers and climbers, lies in the shadow of Ben Nevis → p. 66, Scotland's highest mountain. You can either stop off at Fort William or stay on board. After a short stopover here the train continues its journey further west and passes by the village of Glenfinnan on Loch Shiel. At the lake shore is the solitary Glenfinnan Monument, built in memory of 19 August 1745, the day when Bonnie Prince Charlie arrived here on the shore to begin his campaign to conquer Great Britain – that ended in defeat at the Massacre of Culloden. He survived the battle, returned to the Loch Shiel area and escaped to France. In 1815 a clan leader had the memorial built at the loch – it depicts a valiant

Highlander in a kilt. Another good reason to alight here is the 380m/1246ft long, 30m/98ft high Glenfinnan Viaduct – the scene of numerous film shoots, including the Harry Potter films.

Some five hours further on the line ends in the small fishing town of Mallaig. Your best bet is to stay overnight at the charming West Highland Hotel *(20 rooms | 01687 46 22 10 | Moderate)* where you can enjoy lovely sea views with your dinner. Mallaig is also where you switch your

railway.co.uk) begins. The first part of the journey is a along the coast then the train heads eastwards through the serene isolation of the Central Highlands. The train takes two and a half hours to get to Inverness → p. 68. If you want to explore this buzzing Highlands capital then the centrally located Columba Hotel, right on the River Ness, is a good option *(50 rooms | tel. 01463 23 13 91 | Moderate)*.

From Inverness it is a quick train ride through the Grampian Mountains back

Movie material: even Harry Potter's Hogwarts Express has steamed across Glenfinnan Viaduct

transport and take the ferry (30 min) to Armadale on the island of Skye → p. 80 *(ferry connections: www.calmac.co.uk/ www.kylerailway.co.uk)*. For some breathtaking scenery why not spend a few days exploring Skye before taking the bus across the bridge back to the Scottish mainland town of Kyle of Lochalsh where the single track Kyle Line *(www.kyle*

to Edinburgh. The other option is the north coast. It takes three and a half hours to get to Thurso and the northern Highlands where you are more likely to see red deer than people. Off Thurso are the mysterious Orkneys, a group of islands which are only accessible from here by boat. Flights back to Edinburgh leave daily from Kirkwall on Orkney.

SPORTS & ACTIVITIES

Golf is a hugely popular sport in Scotland. The prices are reasonable so holidaymakers, even beginners, can try their hand at a round while the splendid coasts also draw novice sailors who want to see Scotland from a different perspective.

Be sure to pack your hiking boots for the Highlands and the glens, and you may even want to hire a mountain bike for a cross-country cycle. The countless lakes and rivers are great for anglers and canoers. The *Great Glen Water Park (South Laggan, near Spean Bridge)* outdoor centre offers accommodation and hosts activities including whitewater rafting. *Tel. 07710 54 03 98 | www.monsteractivities.com*

ANGLING

Scotland offers world-class fishing so it is 'tight lines!' on just about all the rivers and lakes. Visitors can enquire at local tourist offices about day licences and they are generally obtainable from the post office or angling clubs. As a rule the fee is around £4 per day for fish such as pike or carp but if it's salmon you're after then spots on the best rivers can command as much as £400. Country hotels often offer their guests free fishing opportunities. Trout fishing is possible between March and October, while the salmon season is from January to October. Famous salmon rivers are the

Photo: St Andrews golf course

Hiking, fishing, golf and sailing: there are many ways to best experience Scotland's nature

Tweed, Spey and Dee, while the many larger Highland lochs are top trout areas: *www.fishing-scotland.net*.

CANOEING & KAYAKING

Countless rivers, 6000 lakes and thousands of miles of coast make for the perfect terrain for both beginner and experienced canoeists. Excellent water sports centres in the small towns of *Elie (Region Fife | tel. 01333 33 09 62)* and *Croft-na-Caber (Loch Tay | tel. 01887 83 05 88)* offer courses and boats. Generally there are camping sites and ample B&Bs on site. The west coast and the Outer Hebrides coastline are particularly recommended – the latter is listed as one of the world's best sea kayaking areas *(www.visithebrides.com/sports/kayaking)*. Try *Uist Outdoor Centre*

(Lochmaddy, North Uist | tel. 01876 50 04 80 | www.uistoutdoorcentre.com) for good equipment and guides, also for beginners. From here you can also get INSIDER TIP sea kayak transport to the remote St Kilda archipelago. A tip for beginners: *Dun Eadinn Sea Kayaking* at the Firth of Forth near Edinburgh offers manageable sea kayaking excursions. You will kayak beneath the famous red railway bridge and to the islands in the Forth. The route is

on a 145km/90mi stretch from Biggar to Berwick-upon-Tweed *(www.bestofthe borders.co.uk)*. The well marked *Great Glen Cycle Route* goes 130km/80mi from Fort William to Inverness. Information on long distance cycling routes: *www.cycle-n-sleep.co.uk*. Best for mountain biking is *Leanachan Forest* in the Nevis range: *Off Beat Bikes | 117 High Street | Fort William | tel. 01397 70 40 08 | www.offbeatbikes. co.uk*

Discover Scotland's pristine nature by going on a hiking trail

rich in bird and seal life. *From 3 hours and £45 | tel. 07786 51 07 71 (mobile) | www. duneideannseakayaking.com*

CYCLING

The quiet and well demarcated cycling routes of the Borders region are perfect for some tranquil – if occasionally hilly – bicycle outings. The INSIDER TIP *4 Abbeys Cycle Route* links all the abbey ruins in a 90km/55mi round trip while the *Tweed Cycle Way* explores the Borders east coast

DIVING

Dive enthusiasts can rent the necessary equipment from dive centres and many also offer courses. Experienced divers will appreciate the spectacular dive off Stromness where INSIDER TIP German shipwrecks from World War I are 50m/ 164ft deep in the Scapa Flow *(Diving Cellar Scapa Flow | tel. 01856 85 03 95 | www.dive scapaflow.co.uk)*. The good underwater visibility around the Outer Hebrides, such as North Uist or at the Summer Isles off

Ullapool, are also ideal conditions for beginners. St Abb's Head near Eyemouth on the east coast is a *marine reserve* which means there is plenty of underwater life here. Find out more through local tourist offices.

GOLF

Just about every town has a golf course and even on the remotest islands you can spend time on the local green from as little as £8. Golf clubs are all open to the general public. For beginners the best options are Scotland's numerous golfing hotels – and it doesn't have to be the famous *Gleneagles* in Perthshire the first time round. Seasoned players who want to tee off on sought after greens like *St Andrews* or *Troon* will be paying £235 upwards and should book months in advance. Info: *www.golf.visitscotland.com*

HIKING

The ⭐ *West Highland Way* (152 km/94mi) from Milngavie (Glasgow) to Ben Nevis at Fort William (*www.west-highland-way. co.uk*) is ideal because it is well signposted and feasible without a tent. The *Southern Upland Way* (350km/217mi) connects Portpatrick in the south of the west coast with St Bathans on the east coast (*www. southernupland.com*). The climb up and down Ben Nevis from Fort William takes a day. The Hebridean island of Skye has superb hiking terrain: easy trails through the moors, strenuous hill walks and challenging climbs in the breathtaking Cuillins Mountains. Organised hikes in small groups that leave from Edinburgh by minibus are offered by the reputable *Walk About Scotland*. Day trips from Edinburgh start at 8am and cost £50. Week-long trips with set dates to an island such as Skye cost from £750 including meals, guided tour, accommodation and transport. *April to Oct. | tel. 0845 6 86 13 44 (*) | www. walkaboutscotland.com*

HORSEBACK RIDING

Discovering Scotland from the saddle of a docile Highland pony is a real treat. Whether you want to do a mountain trek, cross rivers or gallop along the beach, the options in Scotland are endless – even for experienced horse riders. In the north you can try *Highlands Unbridled (Brora | tel. 01408 62 27 89 | www.highlandsunbridled. co.uk)* while *Tomintoul Riding Centre (St Bridget Farm, Ballindalloch | tel. 01807 58 02 10 | www.highlandhooves.co.uk)* covers the Malt Whisky Trail and the Cairngorms National Park. Certified horseback riding clubs: *www.ridinginscotland.com*

SAILING, SURFING & WINDSURFING

The waters between the Inner Hebrides and around Skye make for challenging sailing areas. From Rothesay on the Isle of Bute you can take leisurely day or weekly trips organised by the *Bute Sailing School | Battery Place | Rothesay | tel. 01700 50 48 81*. For information about charters and sailing lessons go to *www.sailscotland. co.uk*.

A good spot for windsurfing and dinghy sailing beginners is Loch Lomond; for the more experienced the west coast is recommended. You can take a one week sailing course with *Tighnabruaich Sailing School (Tighnabruaich | Argyll | tel. 01700 81 17 17 | www.tssargyll.co.uk)*. The conditions at the Mull of Kintyre in Machrihanish and on Lewis are excellent for surfers *(Hebridean Surf Holidays | Stornoway | tel. 01851 70 58 62)*, while the Isle of Tiree – daily by ferry or air *(Loganair)* – has Scotland's best windsurfing conditions.

TRAVEL WITH KIDS

Scotland is an exciting travel destination for children as it is full of forests and moors, and sports and adventure parks.

KELBURN CASTLE (121 D2) (*∅ H13*)

A castle surrounded by a mysterious forest with hiking trails and wild flowing waters. The guided pony rides are a hit with children as is their custom built indoor play area in a wooden fort with slides etc. Appealing wall murals cover the southern side of the old walls. *Largs (A78) | daily from Easter to end Oct 10am–6pm | www. kelburnestate.com | adults £8, children £6*

INSIDER TIP CREAM O'GALLOWAY ☺
(121 F5) (*∅ J15*)

This farm near Rainton in the Galloway region makes delicious ice cream from organic milk. With a huge serving in hand, your children can first view the cattle and sheep enclosures and then amuse themselves in the adventure park which has a high tower that looks across to the Isle of Man. *Near Rainton, south of Gatehouse of Fleet, between Dumfries and Stranraer | March–Oct 10am–6pm | www.creamogalloway.co.uk*

DEEP SEA WORLD (122 C1) (*∅ K12*)

In an old quarry beneath the wonderful *Forth Rail Bridge* is the world's longest underwater tunnel – see seals, rays and colourful fish and from the café you can watch the divers feed the sharks. *North Queensferry 15 minutes by train with the Fife Circle Line from Edinburgh | Mon–Sat 10am–5pm, Sun 10am–4pm | www.deep seaworld.com | adults £10, children £7*

HAUNTED TOURS (127 D6) (*∅ L12*)

Everyone is bound to get goose bumps on one of the *Auld Reekie Tours* such as the evening walks through the alleyways of Edinburgh or a tour of the places where witches gathered or of creepy underground vaults *(45 Niddry St. | tel. 0131 5 57 47 00 | www.auldreekietours.com | adults from £6, children from £4)*. The most informative – and least gruesome – is a tour offered by the guides of *The Real Mary King's Close*. They'll take you on an hour-long walk through the secret warren of streets below the Royal Mile that were closed off because of the plague. *2 Warriston's Close | daily 10am–5pm | www.realmarykingsclose. com | adults £10.50, children £6*

Scotland is one big adventure playground: never a dull moment in the land of castles, ghosts and wild animals

MUSEUM OF CHILDHOOD
(127 D6) (*L12*)

The museum is crammed with toys and the dolls, tin soldiers, old books and model trains are so interesting that your children will not want to leave. *42 High Street, Edinburgh | Mon–Sat 10am–5pm, July/ Aug also Sun noon–5pm | admission free*

WILDLIFE

Puffins, cormorants, dolphins and seals: the best time to watch the wildlife along Scotland's coast is from May to July. Hiking across the Isle of Handa off Scotland's north-west coast is a memorable experience for both children and adults. Rangers from the Scottish Wildlife Trust organise the tour. *Tarbet Pier at Scourie | April–Sept daily 9.30am–5pm | tel. 07920 46 85 72 | www.swt.org.uk | adults £10, children £5).* Great bird watching sites are: *Fowlsheugh Reserve* at Stonehaven/Aberdeenshire;

the cliffs of *Papa Westray* on Orkney Mainland; *Sumburgh Head;* the *Isle of Noss* on the Shetlands; the *Scottish Seabird Centre* in North Berwick and *Bass Rock* island in the south-east. For operators: *www.visit scotland.com/info/wildlife*

WINGS OVER MULL
(124 B–C 4–5) (*E–F 10–11*)

The Hebridean island of Mull is home to many birds of prey, including eagles and owls. The *Conservation Centre*, run by Richard and Sue Dewar, is home to 25 bird species. They give lectures on ornithology and environmental protection and demonstrations of the birds in flight as well as taking guided tours to the south-east of the island. *Auchnacroish House | Torosay | Isle of Mull | Craignure | daily from Easter until end Oct 10.30am–5pm, bird shows noon, 2pm and 4pm | www.wingsovermull. com | adults £4.50, children £1.50*

FESTIVALS & EVENTS

The largest and most important Scottish celebrations are the *Highland Games* that take place from June to Sept around the whole country, but the numerous local folk festivals are even more popular: *www.footstompin.com/articles/festivals*

PUBLIC HOLIDAYS

1 Jan *(New Year's Day)*; **Good Friday**; **last Mon in May** *(Spring Bank Holiday)*; **1st Mon in Aug** *(Summer Bank Holiday)*; **30 Nov** *(St Andrew's Day)*; **25/26 Dec**.

FESTIVALS & LOCAL EVENTS

JANUARY

▶ Second half Jan: INSIDER TIP *Celtic Connection* festival in Glasgow. *www.celticconnections.com*

▶ 25 Jan: *Burns Supper* is celebrated in pubs and restaurants around the country with haggis, whisky and poetry to commemorate the birthday of poet Robert Burns

▶ 31 Jan: *Up Helly Aa* is a fire festival held in Lerwick, Shetland that ends with the ceremonial burning of a Viking boat

APRIL

▶ Beginning April: *Edinburgh International Science Festival*. *www.sciencefestival.co.uk*

▶ Second week: the *Shetland Folk Festival* is a non-profit festival that has been going strong for 30 years. *www.shetlandfolkfestival.com*

MAY

▶ Third weekend: *Orkney Folk Festival*

▶ End May: *Blair Atholl Highlands Gathering* with a parade by the Atholl Highlanders – Scotland's only private army. *www.blairatholl.org.uk*

▶ End May: *Edinburgh Marathon* is the UK's second-largest distance run. *www.edinburgh-marathon.com*

JUNE

▶ Second week: *Folk Festival* in Arran

▶ Mid June: INSIDER TIP *St Magnus Festival* on Mainland Orkney is a week-long festival celebrating classical music and Scottish literature – initiated by composer Sir Peter Maxwell Davies and author George Mackay Brown. *www.stmagnusfestival.com*

▶ End of June: *traditional music festival* in Dingwall

The Scots are always celebrating: here are the best tips on where to see the tossing of the caber and where the whisky flows

▶ Last week: the *Royal Highland Show* in Edinburgh is Scotland's largest agricultural show

JUNE–AUGUST

▶ INSIDER TIP *Common Ridings* take place in many Borders towns: a combination of riding festival, music parade and annual fair that commemorates the tradition of clan boundary riding. *www.scotborders.gov.uk*

JULY

▶ Mid July: the famous *Hebridean Celtic Music Festival* in Stornoway. *www.hebceltfest.com*

▶ End July/beginning August: *Herring Queen Festival* in Eyemouth

AUGUST

▶ ★ *Edinburgh Festival:* for three weeks the entire city becomes a stage for the city's two million festival goers. A must for music and performing arts fans, the *Edinburgh International Festival* is three weeks of concerts and theatre with many international stars *(www.eif.co.uk)*. A springboard for young artists is *The Fringe*, theatre and comedy shows with a contemporary, experimental character *(www.edfringe.com)*. Taking place at the same time is the *Military Tattoo* where military bands perform on a stage in front of the castle. *www.edinburghfestivals.co.uk*

▶ 1st Sunday: *Alternative Games*; in Parton where long lost Scottish games have been revived

SEPTEMBER

▶ First Sat: ★ ● *Highland Games* in Braemar. Traditional event attended by the royal family with disciplines that range from the caber toss to bagpipe competitions. *www.braemargathering.org*

LINKS, BLOGS, APPS & MORE

LINKS

▶ www.nts.org.uk/ThistleCamps If you are a nature lover and don't mind getting your hands dirty then grab a spade and help the non-profit National Trust of Scotland. They offer working holidays on more than 100 properties. You can make a contribution by taking care of the natural environment. So how about gardening and sheep shearing on Fair Isle or doing some drystone walling in Glencoe?

▶ www.guardian.co.uk/edinburgh Topical current affairs contributions about Edinburgh and Scotland, from England's best newspaper

▶ en.wikipedia.org/wiki/Portal Scotland History, politics, geography, culture, architecture and events – here you can find the answers to many a question about Scotland!

▶ www.undiscoveredscotland.co.uk An excellent online resource and guide for accommodation and tourist information. The site has an interactive map so each area is searchable by category

BLOGS & FORUMS

▶ www.edinburghwhiskyblog.com A quirky blog run by two twentysomething whisky connoisseurs from Edinburgh who call themselves 'spirit geeks'! A blog that is a breath of fresh air in the malt world

▶ http://flickr-scotland.blogspot.com A photo weblog that will whet your appetite: photographers regularly post their amazing, artistic photos of Scotland, its people and its landscape

▶ http://scotlandinthegloaming. blogspot.com A brilliant blog project constantly updated with new photos from around Scotland showing twilight and the gloaming – the time of day artists and poets call the blue hour – before sunrise and after sunset

Regardless of whether you are still preparing your trip or already in Scotland: these addresses will provide you with more information, videos and networks to make your holiday even more enjoyable

VIDEOS, STREAMS & PODCASTS

▶ www.youtube.com/watch?v=Lppq DKvxZkI&NR=1&feature=fvwp In just eight minutes you learn a whole lot about the history and production of the Scottish national drink

▶ www.guardian.co.uk/lifeandstyle/ video/2010/sep/06/birds An interesting video about a falconer in the Highlands

▶ www.youtube.com/watch?v=BOs O1wdBhMY A short film about the training of Scottish sheep Border collies, it clearly demonstrates their remarkable instinct for herding and driving

APPS

▶ Cairngorms National Park – GPS Map Navigator The nature reserve's own app gives you up to date information on the weather in the mountains, restaurants and accommodation in addition to detailed route maps for motorists and hikers. It can also help you track down last minute offers if you need somewhere to stay

▶ Ian Rankin's Edinburgh With this free app you can join the crime thriller author on a personal tour of the city of Edinburgh – it includes audio and video extras. Rankin's protagonist, Inspector John Rebus, also features

NETWORK

▶ www.facebook.com/scotlandsforme Numerous tourism companies have joined forces to create this dynamic facebook link that includes events, tourist attractions and last minute offers and personal anecdotes. If Sir Walter Scott, the father of Scottish tourism were alive today, this would be his site of choice

▶ wiki.couchsurfing.org/en/Scotland Want to crash on a local's couch? Couchsurfing is a hospitality exchange and social network so if you're looking for free accommodation for the night the site has listings for all areas. It is even possible to find something for the same night in the larger cities and St Andrews

▶ http://en.homeforhome.com A home exchange site where you can swap your own home for a stay in say, a penthouse in Glasgow, or an apartment on Skye. There are a number of listings for each area in Scotland

TRAVEL TIPS

ACCOMMODATION

Scotland offers a wide range of accommodation options. If you like the idea of a holiday apartment in a castle or an old, historical house then your best bet is the National Trust: *tel. 0131 2 43 93 31 | www.nts.org.uk.* You can find select B&Bs listed at *www.scotlandsbestbandbs.co.uk.* For general accommodation and hotels a good website is *www.visitscotland.com*

If a farm holiday is what you are after then refer to *www.scotfarmhols.co.uk. Holiday Care* is a service that offers holiday tips for people with disabilities and they have a database of more than 1000 suitable hotels, self-catering options, guesthouses and farms: *tel. 0845 124 99 71 (*) | www.holidaycare.org.uk*

ARRIVAL

Scotland has four international airports; Edinburgh, Glasgow, Glasgow Prestwick and Aberdeen. There are direct flights to Scotland from the USA and Canada but those flying in from other countries will need to fly first to London or one of the other European hubs and then take a connecting flight. *Edinburgh Airport (www.edinburghairport.com)* is 12km/7.4mi west of the city centre. The comfortable express bus no. 100 takes you into the city (Princes Street) in about 30 minutes. You purchase your ticket at the bus stop in front of the terminal and not from the driver. Minibuses *(www.edinburghshuttle.com)* leave from the designated car park and will take you to your hotel for £12. The cheapest option is by public service bus no. 35 *(www.lothianbusses.com)* for £3 and if you plan to travel by bus again later on the same day it's worth buying a day ticket for £3. A taxi into the city costs around £18. *Glasgow Prestwick Airport* is about 50km/31mi west of the city centre. Both the bus and train take about an hour to get into town (£4 to £9.50).

There are direct routes to Scottish ports from Northern Ireland and Ireland and indirect routes from Europe via Hull or Newcastle, in north-east England. From Northern Ireland, several companies run regular services (up to 8 times a day) between the Emerald Isle and Scotland. The routes between Belfast and Stranraer (a 2hr crossing), Belfast and Cairnryan (2hrs 15mins) and Larne to Troon (2hrs) are probably the most interesting. For more information on routes and ticket prices: *Stena Line (www.stenaline.co.uk), P&O Ferries (www.poferries.com), DFDS Seaways (www.dfdsseaways.co.uk)* and *Irish Ferries (www.irishferries.com).*

RESPONSIBLE TRAVEL

It doesn't take a lot to be environmentally friendly whilst travelling. Don't just think about your carbon footprint whilst flying to and from your holiday destination but also about how you can protect nature and culture abroad. As a tourist it is especially important to respect nature, look out for local products, cycle instead of driving, save water and much more. If you would like to find out more about eco-tourism please visit: *www.ecotourism.org*

From arrival to weather

Holiday from start to finish: the most important addresses and information for your Scotland trip

There are frequent direct train services from Kings Cross Station in London (every hour) to Edinburgh (www.mytrainticket.co.uk). The journey usually takes around 4 hours and ticket prices vary from £20 to £200, depending on fare. The Glasgow service runs from London Euston and takes about 5 hours. *First ScotRail (www.firstscotrail.com)* also offer an overnight service, the *Caledonian Sleeper* from London Euston to Edinburgh, Glasgow, Stirling, Perth, Dundee, Aberdeen and Inverness. It is advisable to book your train travel well in advance

BANKS & CREDIT CARDS

You can withdraw cash using your EC or debit card at ATMs at the airport and at many locations in the city. Hotels, shops and restaurants will accept the standard credit cards, as will most of the pubs. Banks are open from *9am to 5pm Mon–Fri*, except, of course, on public holidays.

BUS

The bus companies *National Express* and *Scottish Citylink* cover an extensive network. If you're thinking of taking the bus frequently then you should enquire about specials at: *Scottish Citylink Coaches Ltd | tel. 08705 50 50 50 (*) | www.citylink. co.uk*

CAMPING

Scotland has around 500 camp sites. If you're travelling by camper van your best bet is to stay in a holiday park overnight. They usually also have stationary cara-vans for hire. For information on sites and prices go to: *www.visitscotland.com/guide/where-to-stay/camping-caravanning*.
If you want to hire a camper you'll find top of the range models as well as budget options at: *www.coolcampervans.com*. Sites with high quality amenities are given the *Scottish Thistle Award*, a tourism commendation for excellence.

BUDGETING

Whisky	From £20/$33 a bottle
Coffee	£1.80/$3.3 a cup
Taxi	£5.50/$9 for a short trip
Fish & chips	£4/$6.50 from a take-away
Petrol (gas)	£1.10/$1.80 for a litre of regular
Soup	£4/$.6.5 in a pub

Camping out in the wild is not prohibited in Scotland but it is important that you ask permission from the landowner first. If you're thinking of parking your car or camper van somewhere on the side of the road, first make sure that there are not signs prohibiting this.

CLIMATE & WHEN TO GO

Scottish summers are usually quite mild with average temperature of around 70° F/21° C degrees. The mercury will seldom rise to more than 86°F/30°C and seldom drops below 57°F/14°C. In spring and autumn you can expect cool 50°F/10°C degree days. Scottish winters can be cold and rainy although negative temperatures are rare, the Highlands are the exception. Always include warm and rainproof clothing when you pack.

CURRENCY CONVERTER

$	£	£	$
1	0.70	1	1.40
3	2.10	3	4.20
5	3.50	5	7
13	9.10	13	18.20
40	28	40	56
75	52.50	75	105
120	84	120	168
250	175	250	350
500	350	500	700

For current exchange rates see www.xe.com

CONSULATES & EMBASSIES

CONSULATE OF THE UNITED STATES OF AMERICA

3 Regent Terrace | Edinburgh EH7 5BW | tel. +44 13 15 56 83 51 | www.edinburgh.usconsulate.gov

AUSTRALIAN HONORARY CONSULATE

Mitchell House | 5 Mitchell Street | Edinburgh EH6 7DB | tel. +44 13 15 38 05 82 | www.dfat.gov.au/missions/countries/uked.html

CONSULATE OF CANADA

50 Lothian Road | Edinburgh EH3 9WJ | tel. +44 13 14 73 63 20 www.canadainternational.gc.ca/united_ kingdom

CUSTOMS

The allowance when entering Great Britain from countries outside the European Union, including North America, is: 1 litre of spirits, 200 cigarettes or 100 cigarillos or 50 cigars or 250 g of tobacco, 50 g of perfume or 250 g of eau de toilette and other articles (except gold) to a value of £390. For more information: *www.hmrc.gov.uk/customs.* Returning residents of the United States do not have to pay duty on articles purchased overseas up to the value of $800, but there are limits on the amount of alcoholic beverages and tobacco products allowed. For the regulations for international travel for U.S. residents please see *http://www.cbp.gov*

DRIVING IN SCOTLAND

Scotland has a well-developed road network and for tourists from outside of the UK: remember that you drive on the left in the UK. At roundabouts (which are everywhere in Britain) cars coming from the right have the right of way. The speed limit in built-up areas is 30 mph (50 km/h), 60 mph (96 km/h) on unrestricted single carriage roads and 70 mph (112 km/h) on motorways and dual carriageways. Filling stations on the islands and in the Highlands may be closed on a Sunday. Many of the roads on the islands and in the remote Highlands and coastal regions are single track with lay-bys to allow you to pull over to give way to oncoming traffic. An oncoming vehicle will flash their lights to let you know you are being given the right of way.

It costs about £25–£65 a day to hire a car (a valid credit card is required and the minimum age is 21 years). Both Edinburgh and Glasgow airports have several international car hire companies to choose from.

ELECTRICITY

220–240 volts AC. Three-pronged plugs are the norm so you may require an adapter. If you need one they are for sale in many places in Scotland or you can ask at your hotel.

EMERGENCY

Police, fire brigade, ambulance: *tel. 999*, by mobile phone *112*

EVENTS

The daily newspaper 'The Scotsman' *(www.scotsman.com)* publishes the dates and prices for many shows and events. The leading internet entertainment guide is 'The List' *(www.list.co.uk)* or you can go to the national portal *www.ticketmaster.co.uk* (type in Edinburgh in the search field).

FERRIES

The *Caledonian MacBrayne* transports passengers, bicycles and motor vehicles to the Inner and Outer Hebrides off the west coast. In the summer months it is advisable to book your trip in advance *(Caledonian MacBrayne | tel. 0800 066 50 00 | www.calmac.co.uk)*. *North Link Ferries* connects the mainland with Orkney and Shetland on the Scrabster–Stromness and Aberdeen–Kirwall–Lerwick routes *(www.northlinkferries.co.uk)*. In the summer months local ferries commute between Shetland, Mainland and the other islands *(www.poferries.com)*.

HEALTH

For non-UK residents, the European insurance card EHIC *(European Health Insurance Card)* will be accepted by hospitals run by the *National Health Service (NHS)* and

Epitome of a medieval fortress: Caerlaverock Castle

most doctors. In other cases you will have to pay directly and submit your bill for refunding when you return home.

INFORMATION

VISITSCOTLAND

Scotland's national tourism advisory has a wealth of information on accommodation, things to do and general travel information *www.visitscotland.com*.

INFORMATION IN EDINBURGH

Edinburgh & Scotland Information Centre | 3 Princes Street | Edinburgh EH2 2QP | tel. 0845 2 25 51 21 (*)

NEWSPAPERS

The Scottish are patriotic and are very supportive of their own newspapers. In Edinburgh the leading newspaper is 'The Scotsman', in Glasgow it is 'The Glasgow Herald'. Major international newspapers are also available but not always on the day of publication.

OPENING TIMES

Most shops are open Mon–Sat 9am–5.30pm. The larger cities often offer extended shopping hours on a Thursday and are sometimes also open on Sundays. Pubs are generally open until at least 11pm, post offices Mon–Fri 9am–5.30pm, the larger ones also on Saturdays from 9am–12.30pm.

PHONE & MOBILE PHONE

Dialling code to phone the UK from abroad: *+44;* from the UK to: United States and Canada *+1;* Ireland *+353;* Australia *+61* Information: national *tel. 118500;* international: *tel. 118505.*
Phone cards (values: £2–£20) can be purchased at the post office and in shops displaying the BT (British Telecom) symbol. Many phone booths will also accept the standard credit cards.

PRICES & CURRENCY

The currency in Britain is the pound sterling (£) divided into 100 pence (p). The Scots have their own currency, the Scottish pound which is the same value as the sterling (for more information see the chapter 'In a Nutshell') there are 5, 10, 20 and 50 pound notes and uniquely in Scotland also a 1 pound note.

RAIL

Scotland by rail is an attractive alternative because of its scenic landscapes. You can book the *Brit Rail Scottish Freedom Pass* (four or eight days) online at *www.britrail. com* and timetables and routes at *www.*
scotrail.com. It is easy to travel by train in Scotland, the trains travel from Edinburgh along the east coast, through central Scotland and further on all the way up to the ferries to Orkney. The train journey between Edinburgh and Glasgow only takes 50 minutes. From Glasgow you can travel on a very scenic route through Rannoch Moor to Fort William and the Isle of Skye. From Lochalsh on Skye the railway track traverses the Highlands to Inverness. The single carriage wagons generally have a first class section where you will be served coffee free of charge.

TIME

Great Britain is on GMT, *Greenwich Mean Time;* daylight saving time starts and finishes on the same dates as in continental Europe. The North American east coast is 5 hours behind, the west coast 8 hours.

TIPPING

As a rule in Scotland tips are included in the bill. Nevertheless, hotel staff and chambermaids will be appreciative of a small gratuity of say £1 or £2. In restaurants the menu usually states whether or not service is included. If you're happy with the service you should round up by 10 per cent for a tip. The same goes for taxi drivers.

TRAVEL CONCESSIONS

The Explorer Pass from Historic Scotland offers free entry to state attractions and discounts such as for the audio guides in Edinburgh Castle. In addition it saves you having to queue in ticket lines. Historic Scotland is the authority for the conservation of the country's monuments and manages some 360 historical sites such as fortresses, castles and dream destinations like Skara Brae on Orkney. There are two variations of the pass: the three-day pass (£25) which can be used within a period of five days and the seven-day pass (£34) which is valid for a period of 14 days. There are also inexpensive family passes that are valid from the first time you use it. For information and to buy online go to: *www.historic-scotland.gov.uk/explorer.htm*

TRAVELLING WITH DISABILITIES

In recent years Scotland has come a long way to making accommodation options and top tourist attractions, such as castles and fortresses, more accessible for those with disabilities. The Visit Scotland association features attractions with three easy to understand icons for different accessibility levels. For an overview of the wheelchair-friendly accommodation go to: *www.visit scotland.com/guide/where-to-stay/acces sible-scotland*

WEIGHTS & MEASURES

Officially Scotland and Great Britain uses the metric and decimal system but the imperial standards are still in use in every-day life:

1 inch = 2.54 cm; 1 foot = 30.48 cm; 1 yard = 91.44 cm; 1 mile = 1.609 km; 1 ounce = 28.35 g; 1 pound = 453.59 g; 1 pint = 0.5683 l; 1 Imp. gal = 1.2 US liq gal = 4.5459 l.

YOUTH HOSTELS

Many of the youth hostels are in the Highlands, especially in areas popular for sports and activities. You need to be a member of the Scottish Youth Hostels Association and you can apply for this when you arrive. Information: *SYHA National Office | 7 Glebe Crescent, Stirling FK82JA | tel. 01786 89 14 00 | www.syha.org.uk*

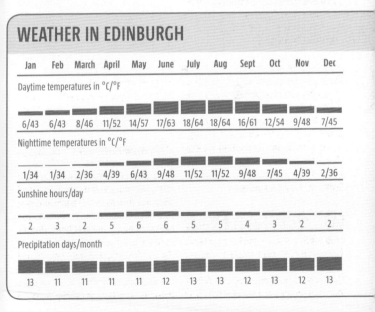

WEATHER IN EDINBURGH

	Jan	Feb	March	April	May	June	July	Aug	Sept	Oct	Nov	Dec
Daytime temperatures in °C/°F	6/43	6/43	8/46	11/52	14/57	17/63	18/64	18/64	16/61	12/54	9/48	7/45
Nighttime temperatures in °C/°F	1/34	1/34	2/36	4/39	6/43	9/48	11/52	11/52	9/48	7/45	4/39	2/36
Sunshine hours/day	2	3	2	5	6	6	5	5	4	3	2	2
Precipitation days/month	13	11	11	11	11	12	13	13	12	13	12	13

NOTES

MARCO POLO TRAVEL GUIDES

MARCO POLO

MARCO POLO

With ROAD ATLAS & PULL-OUT MAP

AKE GARDA

BALDO WITH MOUNTAIN BIKE
at Malcesine bikes takes top

"ES" IN SALÒ
esole ..bacenti

Travel with
**Insider
Tips**

MARCO POLO

With STREET ATLAS & PULL-OUT MAP

EW YORK

, WILD FLOWERS AND SKYSCRAPERS
the High Line in Chelsea

CLOUD NINE
of 220 Fifth Street

Travel with
**Insider
Tips**

MARCO POLO

With ROAD ATLAS & PULL-OUT MAP

FRENCH RIVIERA
NICE, CANNES & MONACO

SPECTACULAR GRAND CANYON DU VERDON
Breath-taking scenery that takes some beating

SNIFFING THE AIR
The perfume manufacturers of Grasse

Travel with
**Insider
Tips**

www.marcopolo.com

MARCO POLO

With STREET ATLAS & PULL-OUT MAP

BERLIN

A STUNNING ISLAND JUST FOR ART
ncreasing treasures from around the world

COOL AT NIGHT
lin club scene sets the trend

Travel with
**Insider
Tips**

MARCO POLO

With ROAD ATLAS & PULL-OUT MAP

ALLORCA

AN FLAIR IN THE MEDITERRANEAN
llorca's most beautiful beach

IN" CROWD MEET
oods in Deià

Travel with
**Insider
Tips**

- PACKED WITH INSIDER TIPS
- BEST WALKS AND TOURS
- FULL-COLOUR PULL-OUT MAP
  AND STREET ATLAS

ROAD ATLAS

The green line   indicates the Trips & Tours (p. 94–99)
The blue line   indicates The perfect route (p. 30–31)

All tours are also marked on the pull-out map

Photo: Kelso on the River Tweed

Exploring Scotland

The map on the back cover shows how the area has been sub-divided

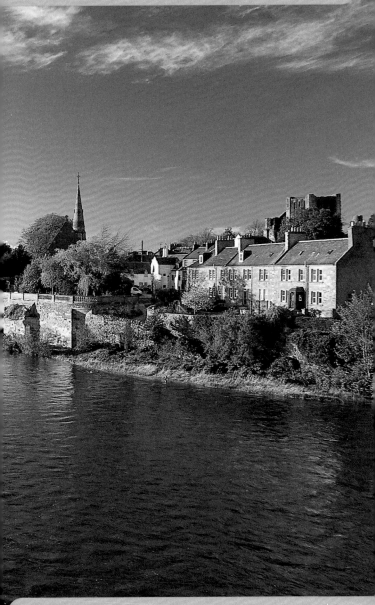

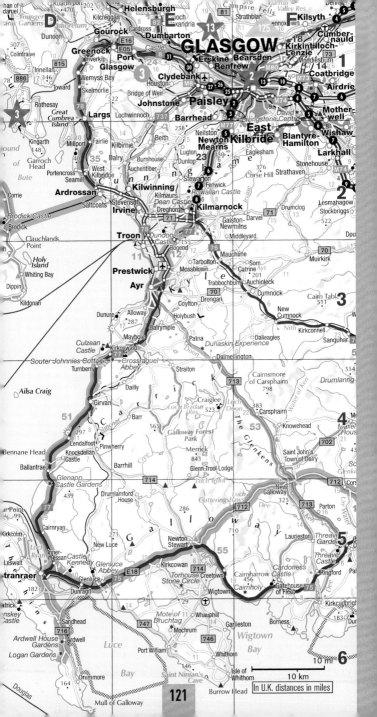

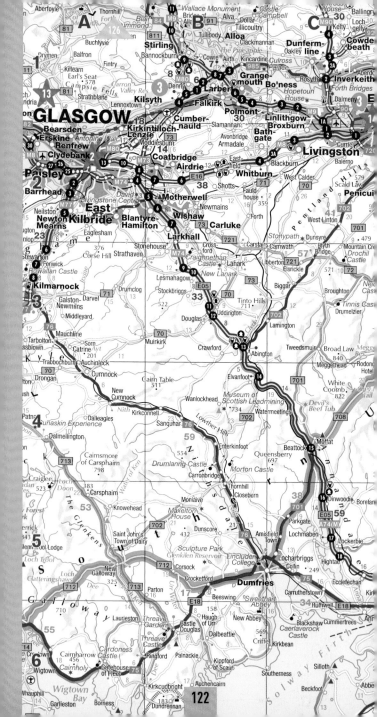

A   **B**   **C**

1

2

3

4

5

6

Idrigill Point · Wiay · Fiskávaig · Drynoch · 863 · Sconser · Peinchorran · Crowlin Islands

Sk y e · Merkadale · Talisker Distillery · Sligachan Hotel · Crofters' Museum House · Scalpay · Kyle of Lo · Pabay · Ky · Hous

M i n g i n i s h · Cuillin Hills · Lui · Broadford · Torrin · 87 · Skular

Glenbrittle House · Sgurr Alasdair △ 993 · Loch Coruisk · 851

Soay · Loch Scavaig · Loch Slapin · Elgol · 299 · Isle

Prince Charles's Cave · Knock Castle

Lochboisdale · Loch Baghasdail

Canna · Magnetic Hill · 211 · Sound of Canna · Armadale Castle & Clan Donald Centre · Má

Sanday · A'Bhrideanach · Kinloch Castle · Aird of Sleat · Point of Sleat

Oigh-sgeir · Rum Rhum · Askival 812 · Sound of Rhum · Glenancross · Bunacaimb · Arisa · 830

Cleadale · 394 · Eigg · Rubh'·Arisaig · Sound o of Arisaig

Castlebay · Muck · 861

Point of Ardnamurchan · Eilean Shona · Ardtoe · Ac

Achosnich · A r d n a m u r c h a n · Salen · Ockle · 528 · Glenborrodale · 512 · Kilchoan · Oronsay · Carna

Sorisdale · Arnabost · Tobermory · Drimnin · M o r

Ballyhaugh · Arinagour · Calgary · Dervaig · 292 · 550 · Arileod · Caliach Point · Coll · 10

Caoles · 256 · Achleck · Salen · 849 · Fishnish · Du · Gha · 766 · 7

Clachan Mór · Scarinish · Loch Tuath · 424 · Crossapol · Treshnish Islands · Gometra · 155 · 313 · Balnahard · 21 Ben More · 18

Barrapol · 141 · Tiree · Staffa · Inchkenneth · Ulva · Loch na Keal · M u l l

Fingal's Cave · 10 · Chapel · Ardmeanach · The Burgh · M 967 · Lochbuie · 405

Abbey · Iona · Baile Mór · Fionnphort · Bunessan · 849 · Carsaig · Loch Buie

Benedictine Nunnery · Ross of Mull · 20 · 376 · Carsaig Arches · Fi

Erraid · 25

Carvellac · Sc

Kilioran Gardens · 43 · Colonsay · Scalasaig · Jura · 477

Oronsay · 93 · Port Askaig · 846

Rubh · a' Mhail · Loch

Sea of the Hebrides

S e a   o f   t h e   H e b r i d e s

H e b r i d e s

M i n c h

10 mi · 10 km · In U.K. distances in miles

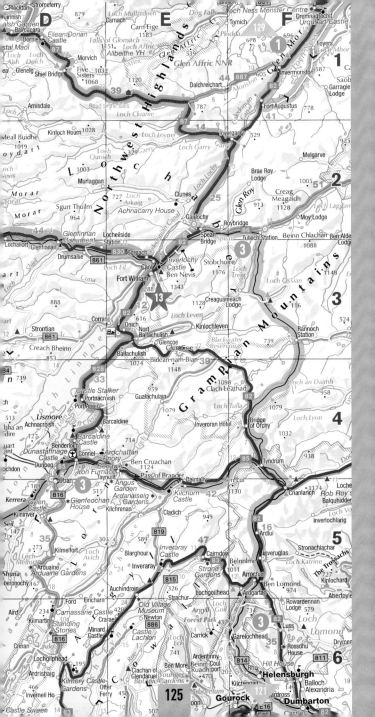

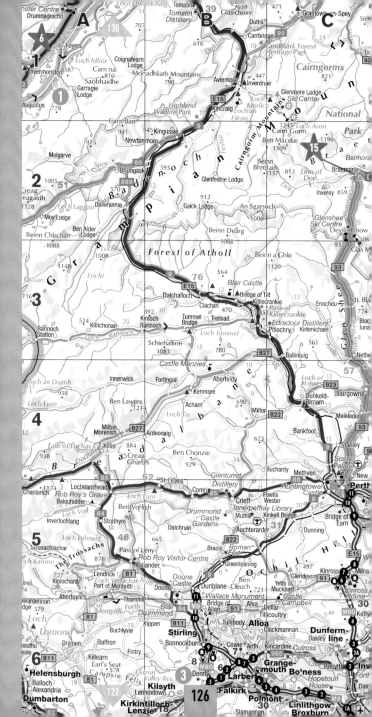

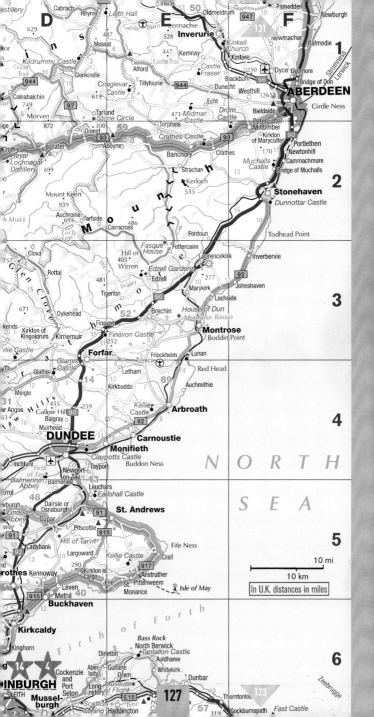

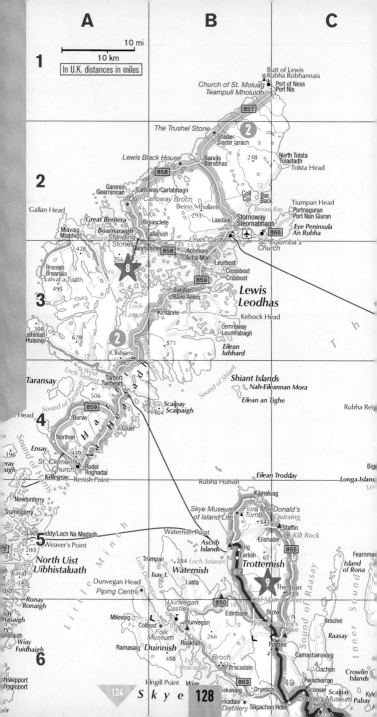

10 mi
10 km
In U.K. distances in miles

Butt of Lewis
✶Rubha Robhannais
Port of Ness
Port Nis
Church of St. Moluag
Teampull Mholuidh
857

The Trushel Stone
✶ Shader
Siadar Iarach

North Tolsta
Tolastadh
Tolsta Head

Lewis Black House
858
Barvas
Barabhas
248

2

Garenin
Gearrannan
Carloway/Carlabhagh
Dun Carloway Broch
Beinn Mholach
291
Coll
Col
Bac
Back

Tiumpan Head
Portnaguran
Port Nan Giuran

Gallan Head
Great Bernera
Boarmaraigh
Standing Stones
Breasclete
Callanish
Stornoway
Steornabhagh
866
Eye Peninsula
An Rubha

Miavaig
Miabhig
Laxdale
Lews Castle
St Columba's Church

Garynahine
858
Achmore
Acha Mor
Leurbost

428
256
⭐ 8

Crossbost
Crosbost
859

Brenish
Breanais
Laival a Tuath
495

Balallan
Baile Ailein

Lewis
Leodhas

Cushinish
Huisinis
679

Kintarvie
Kebock Head

Lemreway
Leumrabagh

308

571

Eilean
Iubhard

⭐ 2

Clisham
799

Sound of Shiant

Shiant Islands
Nah-Eileannan Mora

West
Loch Tarbert
506
Tarbert
Tairbeart
104
Scalpay
Scalpaigh
Eilean an Tighe

Taransay
Sound of Taransay
859
Borve
Northon
Cluer

Rubha Rei

Ensay
459
St. Clements
Church
Rodel
Roghadal
Killegray
Renish Point

Eilean Trodday

Rubha Hunish

Longa Island

Newtonferry
Trumisgarry
Loch Maddy/Loch Na Madadh
Weaver's Point
280

Skye Museum
of Island Life
Flora MacDonald's
Tomb
Kilmaluag
Quiraing
543
Staffin
Kilt Rock
855

North Uist
Uibhistaluath
Waternish Point
Ascrib
Islands
Uig
Earlish
611
Elishader

Fearnmo
Island of Rona

Newtonferry
Trumisgarry
87
Trotternish
⭐ 9

Ronay
Ronaigh
Trumpan
284 Loch Snizort
Isay I.
Waternish
Lusta
Dunvegan Head
Piping Centre

The Storr
719
Old-Man-of-Storr
Prince Charles's Cave

Brochel
Raasay

Wiay
Fuidhaigh
Dunvegan
Castle
Milovaig
Colbost
Folk
Museum
Dunvegan
Roskhill
266
Edinbane
850
Brove

Ramasaig
Duinnish
488
Loch
Bracadale
Broch
Bracadale
Portree

Camastianavaig
Clachan
Crowlin
Islands
Peinchorran
Scalpay
Pabay

Idrigill Point
Wiay
124 ◢ S k y e 128
863
Distillery
Drynoch
Sligachan Hotel
49
Crofter's Museum
House

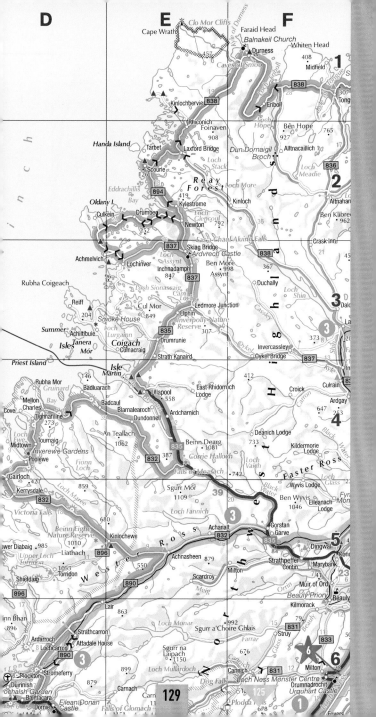

Clo Mor Cliffs
Cape Wrath
Faraid Head
Balnakeil Church
Whiten Head
457
Durness
Midfield
408
Caves of Smoo
1
838
28
Tong
307
Kinlochbervie
838
19
Eriboll
Rhiconich
Ben Hope
Foinaven
927
765
908
Handa Island
Tarbet
Dun Dornaigil
Broch
Alltnacaillich
Laxford Bridge
Loch
Stack
Loch
Meadie
836
Scourie
126
Reay
Forest
Altnaharr
894
419
Eddrachillis
Bay
Kylesku
Loch More
2
Ben Klibre
962
Oldany I.
Drumbeg
Kylestrome
Kinloch
Culkein
241
252
Loch
Glencoul
792
Crask Inn
Newton
36
21
Easan Chaul Aluinn Falls
837
Skiag Bridge
838
367
Achmelvich
Ardvrech Castle
Duchally
Lochinver
Inchnadamph
Ben More
847
Assynt
837
998
Loch
Shin
Loch Assynt
3
Dal
Rubha Coigeach
96
Loch Sionascaig
Cam Loch
Reiff
204
Cul Mor
Ledmore Junction
373
La
Smoke House
849
Cassley
In
835
Elphin
Inverpolly Nature
Reserve
Achiltibuie
Loch
Lurgainn
307
Summer
Tanera
Mór
Coigach
Drumrunie
Invercassley
837
Priest Island
Culnacraig
Strath Kanaird
Oykel Bridge
Isle
Martin
146
412
Culrain
Rubha Mor
Gruinard
East Rhidorroch
Lodge
Croick
Ardgay
647
Mellon
Bay
Ullapool
558
4
Charles
Badluarach
Badcaul
Ardcharnich
Carron
Black Water
Cove
Tighnafiline
273
Blarnalearoch
Dundonnell
Deanich Lodge
733
Kildermorie
Lodge
An Teallach
1062
835
Loch
Ewe
Midtown
Tournaig
Beinn Dearg
1081
Poolewe
832
387
Corrie Halloch
Loch
Vaich
742
Inverewe Gardens
Falls of Measach
Wyvis Lodge
Gairloch
Loch
421
859
Sgurr Mòr
Ben Wyvis
Eileanach
Kerrysdale
1109
1046
Lodge
832
39
20
Fyr
Mon
Victoria Falls
178
Loch Fannich
5
Beinn Eighe
680
Achanalt
Gorstan
Dingwall
Nature Reserve
Kinlochewe
832
Garve
er Diabaig
985
1010
835
84
23
Upper Loch
Liathach
896
Strathpeffer
Marybank
Torridon
1053
Achnasheen
879
Contin
Torridon
550
890
Milton
Muir of Ord
Shieldaig
Meig
Orrin
Beauly Priory
896
Lair
863
Kilmorack
Beauly
inn Bhan
Loch Monar
992
831
896
Sgurr a'Choire Ghlais
79
17
Ardarroch
Farrar
Struy
833
Strathcarron
676
Attadale House
6
890
Sgurr na
Laipach
Milton
Plockton
Lochcarron
899
Cannich
831
12
Stromeferry
Loch Mullardoch
Dog Fall
129
125
Duirinish
879
Carnach
Loch Ness Monster Centre
ochalsh Garden
Drumnadrochit
Balmacara
Urquhart Castle
Dornie
Eilean Donan
Castle
678
Falls of Glomach
Plodda Fa

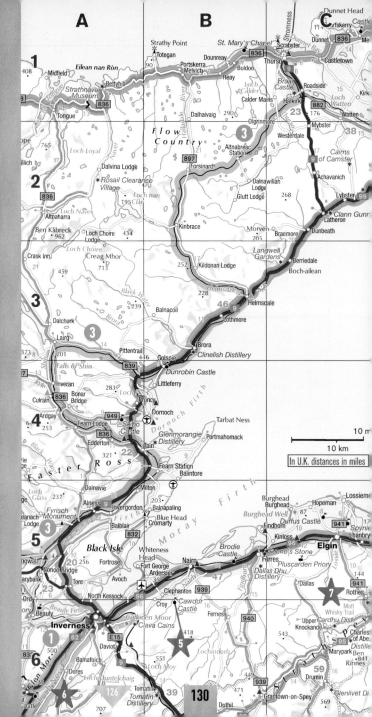

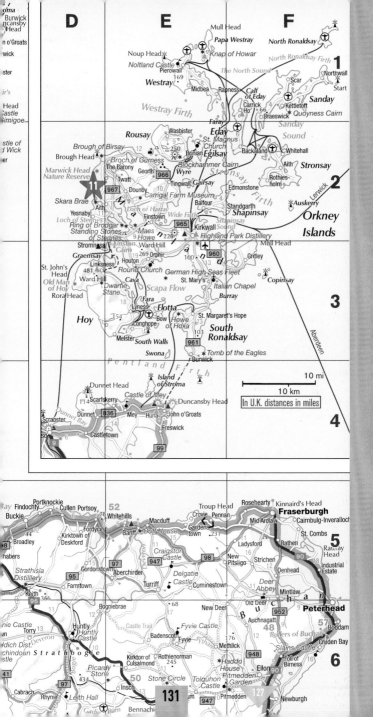

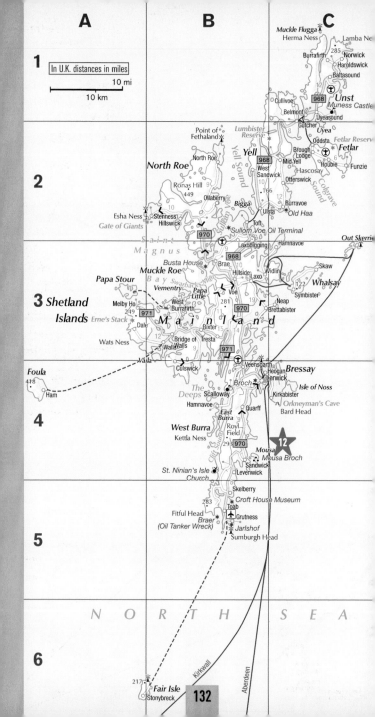

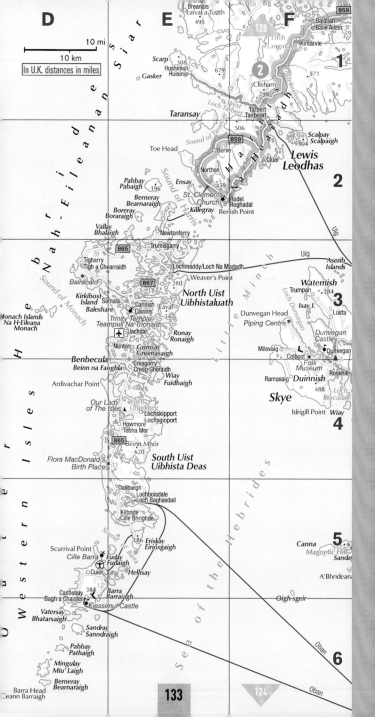

University Aven??
University
Eldon St.
Woodlands
Park
Hunterian
Museum
University
of Glasgow
Park Drive
W. Prince's St.
Cromwell Road
Bu??
Ter.
M
Park
University
of Glasgow
Kelvingrove
Park Circus Lane
Westend Park Street
Arlington Street
Grant St.
Carnarvon St.
Ballol St.
George's Rd
Glasgow Art
Gallery - Museum
Park
Circus
Ashley St.
Lynedoch St.
Woodside
Ter. Lane
Woodside Terrace
St.
Museu
Royal
Highla
Fusilie
KELVINGROVE
Park
Gdns.
18
Newton Street
Sauchiehall Street
Parkgrove
Ter.
Royal Terrace
Clifton St.
Woodside Pl. Lane
Ba??
Argyle
Street
Royal Crs.
Kelvingrove St.
Sauchiehall Street
Sandyford Place La.
Berkeley Street
Char
Cro
St.
Fitzroy Lane
St. Vincent Crescedens Lane
St. Vincent Crescent
Street
Kent Road
North
Dover Street
Dorset St.
n Street
Minerva
Way
The Summ??
Center
Minerva
Street
Street
St. Vincent Street
Elliot St.
St.
St.
Pointhouse Rd.
ross Road
S
Finnieston
Elliot
Elliot
St. Vincent Street
Argyle Street
Street
19
Scottish Exhibition
and Conference
Centre
'Clyde Auditorium'
P
Finnieston
Stobcross Street
S
ss Road
Congress Road
P
Lancefield
Quay
Elliot Street
Lancefield St.
Hydepark Street
Whitehall St.
Warroch St.
Cheapside St.
Washington St.
P
M
S
A
Bell's
Bridge
4
Glasgow
Science
Centre
rive
River Clyde
Anderston
Quay
Bro
Govan Road
Graigiehall
St.
Mavisbank
Gdns.
Odeon
Cinema
Springfield
Quay
Kingston Bridge
TR
Govan Road
Lorne St.
Blackburn St.
Mair St.
Paisley
Watt St.
Houston St.
Mor
Paisley
Road
West
Seaward St.
20
Kinning
Park
M
Cornwall St.
Milnpark St.
Sussex St.
Middlesex St.
Portman St.
Stanley St.
College
Strathclyde
Business Cen
Scotland St.
21
Kinning St.
Carmoustie St.
Gloucester
Laidlaw St.
M8
M
Scotland
durham
Street
Vermont St.
134
St.
Museum
of Education

Glasgow

400 m
400 yds.

DUNDAS

Craighall Rd.

Dobbie's

W. Graham St.
Swimming Pool
City Road
New City Road
Stow College
City Road
Buccleuch La.
Scott St.
Dalhousie St.
Renfrew St.
Rose St.
Cowcaddens
Garscube Road
Maitland Street
Port Dundas Road
Milton Street
McPhater St.
Tyndrum Street
Passport Office Glasgow

Kyle St.
Calgay St.
Cowper St.
Kennedy

Caledonian University

Mackintosh School
Chiehall St.
Chiehall Lane
Pitt St.
McLellan Gall.
Theatre Royal
Sauchiehall St.
Kelvin Gallery
The Pavilion
Caledonian University

Road
Omnibus Station
Killermont St.
Royal Concert Hall
Buchanan Galleries

Necropolis
College
Cathedral Street

West Police Station West Police Bus.
Douglas St.
Blythswood
Regent
West Regent Lane
George Street
Bath Street
West George Lane
Hope Street
Renfield Street
Nile Street
West Street
Bath St.
Queen Street Station
University

Collins Gallery

St. Vincent Lane
Bothwell St.
Bothwell Lane
Wellington
St. Vincent
Pl.
W. George Sq. City Chambers

Waterloo St.
Cadogan
Wellington Lane
Street
Holm St.
Gordon St.
Union Street
St. Vincent Pl.
Royal Ex Sq.
Gallery Modern

W. George Sq. City Chambers
Cochrane St.
Hutchesons Hall
Sheriff Court
Merchant City
Ingram
City Hall

Argyle St.
Central Station
Hope St.
Mitchell St.
Buchanan St.
Queen St.
Miller St.
Virginia St.
Wilson
Brunswick
Street
Bell St.

Argyle St.
Osborne St.
Argyle St.
Trongate

Broomielaw
George V Bridge
Jamaica St.
Howard Street
University
Fox St.
Howard St.
Stockwell St.
Tron Theatre

Clyde
Glasgow Bridge
St. Andrews Cathedral
Bridgegate
Saltmarket
Steel St.

Clyde Place
Bridge St.
Carlton Place
Victoria Bridge
Justiciary Buildings
Peoples Palace

Kingston St.
Glasgow City Council
Nelson St.
Commerce Centre
Oxford St.
Sheriff Court
Adelphi St.
Central Mosque
Crown Street
Albert Bridge
Glasgow Green

Cook Street
Works Tradeston Store
Coburg St.
Portland St.
Bedford St.
Norfolk St.
Ballater Street
Florence Street Clinic

135

KEY TO ROAD ATLAS

Motorway with junctions
Autobahn mit Anschlussstellen

Motorway under construction
Autobahn in Bau

Toll station
Mautstelle

Roadside restaurant and hotel
Raststätte mit Übernachtung

Roadside restaurant
Raststätte

Filling-station
Tankstelle

Dual carriage-way with
motorway characteristics
with junction
Autobahnähnliche Schnell-
straße mit Anschlussstelle

Trunk road
Fernverkehrsstraße

Thoroughfare
Durchgangsstraße

Important main road
Wichtige Hauptstraße

Main road
Hauptstraße

Secondary road
Nebenstraße

Railway
Eisenbahn

Car-loading terminal
Autozug-Terminal

Mountain railway
Zahnradbahn

Aerial cableway
Kabinenschwebebahn

Railway ferry
Eisenbahnfähre

Car ferry
Autofähre

Shipping route
Schifffahrtslinie

Route with
beautiful scenery
Landschaftlich besonders
schöne Strecke

Alleenstr. Tourist route
Touristenstraße

XI-V Closure in winter
Wintersperre

Road closed to motor traffic
Straße für Kfz gesperrt

8% Important gradients
Bedeutende Steigungen

Not recommended
for caravans
Für Wohnwagen nicht
empfehlenswert

Closed for caravans
Für Wohnwagen gesperrt

Important panoramic view
Besonders schöner Ausblick

* Wartenstein Of interest: culture - nature
* Umbalfälle Sehenswert: Kultur - Natur

Bathing beach
Badestrand

National park, nature park
Nationalpark, Naturpark

Prohibited area
Sperrgebiet

Church
Kirche

Monastery
Kloster

Palace, castle
Schloss, Burg

Mosque
Moschee

Ruins
Ruinen

Lighthouse
Leuchtturm

Tower
Turm

Cave
Höhle

Archaeological excavation
Ausgrabungsstätte

Youth hostel
Jugendherberge

Isolated hotel
Allein stehendes Hotel

Refuge
Berghütte

Camping site
Campingplatz

Airport
Flughafen

Regional airport
Regionalflughafen

Airfield
Flugplatz

National boundary
Staatsgrenze

Administrative boundary
Verwaltungsgrenze

⊖ Check-point
Grenzkontrollstelle

⊖ Check-point with
restrictions
Grenzkontrollstelle mit
Beschränkung

ROMA Capital
Hauptstadt

VENÉZIA Seat of the administration
Verwaltungssitz

Trips & Tours
Ausflüge & Touren

Perfect route
Perfekte Route

★ MARCO POLO Highlight
MARCO POLO Highlight

INDEX

This index lists all sights, museums and destinations, plus the names of important people and key words featured in this guide. Numbers in bold indicate a main entry.

DOS & DON'TS ☝

The Scots are neither stingy nor English

DON'T STOP ILLEGALLY

Scotland's landscape makes it tempting for campers to park the car and camp wherever there is a scenic view. The lay-bys on single track roads can be especially inviting, these are not suitable sites to overnight and you'll be endangering both yourself and traffic if you do. The same goes for camping at picnic spots: look out for signs prohibiting camping.

DON'T WAIT FOR YOUR BEER IN THE BAR

If you expect to be waited on and have your beer served at your table you could wait forever. In Scotland you have to order your beer at the bar counter and wait to collect it (and pay for it) there.

DO COME PROPERLY EQUIPPED

Time and again rangers have to rescue reckless tourists from Scotland's national parks and mountain regions. The weather can take a turn for the worse very quickly you should only go hiking or mountain climbing with the appropriate clothing and equipment.

DON'T FISH WITHOUT A LICENSE

Don't let the isolation deceive you, fishing without a license can turn out to be a costly mistake. Most of the rivers and lochs are on private property and require a fishing licence. Ignore the rules and you could be faced with a hefty fine!

DO REMEMBER THE MOSQUITO REPELLENT

Mosquito season is from May to June when these small irritating insects are drawn to water and invade the coastlines in their thousands. Without the proper protection camping and hiking can be a disaster but fortunately all good chemists sell insect repellent.

DON'T CALL THE SCOTS ENGLISH

Not only is this impolite but also incorrect. The Scots are independent and have had their own parliament since 1999. Given Scotland's turbulent history, every Scot will feel offended if you call them English.

DON'T BELIEVE THE CLICHÉ

To this day the Scots are still considered to be stingy yet you would be hard pressed to find a more hospitable nation or one that donates more to worthy causes.

DO GIVE THE FOOD A CHANCE

Fish & chips and nothing more? Wrong! Scotland is no longer a culinary wasteland and now boasts excellent gourmet restaurants. However, they do come at a price so if you enjoy eating well you should make provision for them in your travel budget.

WRITE TO US

e-mail: info@marcopologuides.co.uk

Did you have a great holiday?
Is there something on your mind?
Whatever it is, let us know!
Whether you want to praise, alert us
to errors or give us a personal tip –
MARCO POLO would be pleased to
hear from you.
We do everything we can to provide the
very latest information for your trip.

Nevertheless, despite all of our authors'
thorough research, errors can creep in.
MARCO POLO does not accept any
liability for this. Please contact us by
e-mail or post.

MARCO POLO Travel Publishing Ltd
Pinewood, Chineham Business Park
Crockford Lane, Chineham
Basingstoke, Hampshire RG24 8AL
United Kingdom

PICTURE CREDITS
Cover photograph: The Castle Stalker: Getty Images/Aurora: Santos; Birds flying: Getty Images/Workbook Stock: Henly
BTCV (17 bottom); DuMont Bildarchiv: Modrow (85, 88), Mosler (2 bottom, 29, 52/53, 93, 105); Das Fotoarchiv:
Dlouhy (74), Horwath (94/95); Getty Images/Aurora: Santos (1 top), Workbook Stock: Henly (1 top); Huber: Schmid
(24/25), Giovanni Simeone (71); Hud yer Wheesht: Erin McElhinney (16 bottom); H. Krinitz (front flap r., 2 top,
2 centre top 2 centre bottom, 3 top, 3 centre, 3 bottom, 4, 5, 6, 7, 10/11, 13, 14/15, 18/19, 20/23, 22, 26 left, 27, 28,
28/29, 32/33, 34, 36, 38, 40, 42/43, 44, 49, 51, 54, 56, 61, 62/63, 64, 67, 68, 73, 74/75, 76/77, 78, 81, 83, 86/87,
89, 90, 96, 97, 100/101, 102, 104, 104/105, 106, 106/107, 107, 108 top, 108 bottom, 109, 113, 122/123, 137);
mauritius images: Alamy (front flap left, 8, 30 top, 30 bottom, 46), Phototake (9); Nae Limits: Rezolution Media
– Richard Steel (16 centre); Scotland by Camper Ltd: David Campbell (17 top); The Scottish Fashion Awards: Hartmann
Media (16 top); T. Stankiewicz (26 right, 59)

1st Edition 2013
Worldwide Distribution: Marco Polo Travel Publishing Ltd, Pinewood, Chineham Business Park,
Crockford Lane, Basingstoke, Hampshire RG24 8AL, United Kingdom. Email: sales@marcopolouk.com
© MAIRDUMONT GmbH & Co. KG, Ostfildern
Chief editors: Michaela Lienemann (concept, managing editor), Marion Zorn (concept, text editor)
Author: Martin Müller; editor: Andrea Mertes
Programme supervision: Ann-Katrin Kutzner, Nikolai Michaelis, Silwen Randebrock
Picture editor: Gabriele Forst
What's hot: wunder media, Munich
Cartography road atlas & pull-out map: © MAIRDUMONT, Ostfildern
Design: milchhof : atelier, Berlin; Front cover, pull-out map cover, page 1: factor product munich
Translated from German by Birgitt Lederer; editor of the English edition: Margaret Howie, fullproof.co.za
Prepress: M. Feuerstein, Wigel